LIVING IN THE HOLLOW

William McDaniel McCollum

How far you go in life depends on your being tender with the youth, compassionate with the aged, sympathetic with the striving and tolerant of the weak and the strong...Because someday you will have been all of these.

—**George Washington Carver**

Foreword

I was barefooted and my britches had holes and patches. One of my classmates in school told me that he felt sorry for me because I was poor. I thought I was doing pretty good. I had two egg-and-biscuit sandwiches in my brown paper sack for my lunch. I was healthy, was eating pretty darn good, and I was happy. How could anyone say I was poor? I was not poor; I was blessed.

My first book, *Rural Route One*, is the true life story about the first sixteen years of my life living along the country dirt roads in Morgan County, Alabama. Living and growing up as a sharecropper's son—the hard work and lessons learned—the foundation of my life was formed there. I cannot believe how blessed I was. How blessed that I had a home, parents, and the best brothers and sisters ever. I lived and grew up with some wonderful neighbors who encouraged me, who cared about me, and who wanted me to succeed in this thing called life.

Wonderful memories might just be the best part of life as you can relive them for as long as you live. This book is about those yesterday years, true stories of life and events. Come walk with me down these's dusty dirt roads, I will do my best to make you smile. *Living in the Hollow: Memories of Rural Route One.*

Thank you all for purchasing my books; thank you for borrowing them from a friend or neighbor. But more so, thank you for all the kind words, the wonderful comments; they mean so much more to me than I can ever express to you in words.

William McDaniel McCollum

Contents

1

OUR LANDLORD

A wild ride

Our dad, Conley, and I were walking back home. We had just been to the small country store at Ryan. Back then we walked everywhere and, most every Saturday afternoon, we went to the store to get things we needed. We lived on Mr. Dewitt Crawford's place at the bottom of what was then called the Crawford Shoot. We lived in a really wonderful old house. It was called the "Old Crawford Home Place." Anyway, my dad and I each had a paper sack full of groceries that he had bought at the Ryan store. We were just taking our time as Conley was only four years old and a slow walker, and me at five not much faster. In 1946, the roads were still dirt with some gravel and mostly one lane. They were dusty and rough and, back then, there was not much traffic.

We were just taking our time when all at once we could hear a vehicle coming up behind us; it was really going fast, it seemed. We got off the road as our dad did not want us to get run over by a mad man. It passed us and the dust went everywhere. What was that driver thinking? Then all at once the driver slammed on the brakes and the truck slid to a stop. More dust. He backed up and then asked if we wanted a ride home. Dad put the two bags of groceries in the back and helped us climb in. It was a fun ride as the wind and the dust were blowing in our faces. We were sitting on the floor in the back of this 1941 Ford pick-up truck. As the driver came to the top of a large hill and started down, the truck was really going fast and it was a bumpy ride.

I looked over at Conley and he was a happy looking kid with a big smile. Heck, I was scared as the truck was really going fast. One of the grocery sacks tipped over and the canned pork and beans were rolling around in the back of that pick-up truck. I was holding on for dear life as we were about halfway down. We hit a big bump and more canned goods were spilling out and rolling around in the back. I was hoping that Conley could hang on and not be bounced out of the back of the truck. Out of the corner of my eye I could see he still had a big ole grin on his face, as if he was having the time of his life. I was thinking we were going a hundred miles per hour, or it seemed like it.

We finally made it to the bottom of the hill and then made a sharp turn and slid to a quick stop in the small driveway that led to our house. By this time, all the things that were in the paper sacks were all over the bed of the truck. We got all the stuff put back in the bags and our dad helped us out. Conley still had a grin on his face; his hair was all blown every which way. We both had road dust all over us.

The fellow who was driving this truck was a reckless driver for sure. He asked if we enjoyed the ride; Conley stood there with that happy look on his face. Then he turned to me and asked me what happened as he looked at the front of my pants. I looked down and realized I had peed on myself! I could not believe I did that! I didn't remember doing such a thing. I was beside myself. The driver just laughed as he drove away to check the cattle and sheep that were across the road from where we lived.

That was the very first time that I remember meeting our land-lord, Mr. Dewitt Crawford. I had just had the scariest ride of my life in the back of his truck as he let it coast down the famous steep hill called "The Crawford Shoot." I have to admit that my first impression of him left a lot to be desired. First, he thought it was funny that I had peed on myself and, second, I was thinking he really tried to scare us with that wild, fast, dusty, windy ride down that steep hill. I had made up my mind that I never wanted to ride in the back of another pick-up truck when he was the driver.

Printed sacks

Mr. Dewitt Crawford always brought fertilizer for us in cloth sacks so my mom could make shirts, dresses, towels, diapers, and other things from those cloth fertilizer sacks. I know it had to cost more, but he knew that there were so many uses for the cloth sacks. At first, the sacks were just white or an off-white with the numbers painted on them in red, like 4-10-7 or 12-12-12. Later, the sacks were in different colors. Early in the spring the big truck would come to our house, back up to the barn, and we would unload hundreds of cloth sacks. Some would be in stripes, others in checkered prints, and others in wildflower prints. One time as Mr. Dewitt and my dad were talking, he asked what kind of printed fertilizer sacks my mom wanted. Our dad said it didn't matter. Mr. Dewitt said, "Oh, yes, it does! You better check with the missus." He remembered the last time that my mom was not happy with the printed sacks, and he had heard all about that. So it was decided it would be the blue striped sacks this year. A week or so went by then a large truck came, and we unloaded them out at the barn. Later my mom asked me if it was the blue striped sacks. I was thinking I could have a little fun here. I told her that all the sacks were in pink polka dots. She just looked at me and went right back into the kitchen. About that time our dad came in the back door. Before I could tell her that I was just kidding, she lit into him. She was waving her hands and saying, "I told you this," and "I told you that." Dad was just looking at her, wondering what in the world she was talking about. He told her that all the sacks were blue striped…just what she had asked for. Mom looked at me, and for a moment I thought this was going to be the last day on earth for me! It was a good thing that Mr. Dewitt was not there. Well, maybe I kinda wished he was. I almost got a whopping for something that I was just having some fun with. I was going to tell Mr. Dewitt about that, but I had second thoughts as he might not think that it was as funny as I thought it was. Thinking back, I wish I had told him because he always liked a good laugh.

A blind horse

One of my friends told me about a horse that I could buy for twenty-five dollars, and I thought that was a really good deal. I had always wanted a horse; all we had were mules. I did not like mules. Our dad liked mules. Mr. Dewitt Crawford liked mules. Mules were easy to work with because they were kind of slow yet strong and easy to handle. Usually, they did not get very excited. I wanted a horse to ride even if it was a work horse. Mr. Bolding, who lived up the road from us, had two really nice work horses and they did a good job for him. Why couldn't we have one?

This horse for only twenty-five dollars was a bargain; the only problem was I didn't have the twenty-five dollars. In fact, I didn't even have a dollar. But I did have an old bicycle worth about five dollars at the most. And the real problem was that the filly was blind. I was told if the people who owned her could not find a buyer, she would be taken to the soap factory or the glue factory.

I just had to make a trip down to their farm and look at this horse. One afternoon after I got all my chores done, I rode my bicycle about five miles to see what she looked like. I was about fourteen years old by then. When I got there, only the farmer's wife was home. She took me out into the pasture where the filly was grazing. This horse was a very pretty animal and she was just a pet. The lady told me to start talking to her so I would not scare her. I walked up to her and started petting and rubbing her nose. I gave her a handful of hay and fell in love with her.

Now I had to start using every kind of salesmanship I could muster. I had no money, only an old bicycle, but I really wanted that horse, even though she was blind—maybe more so because she was blind. I asked if I could trade my bicycle for her; that did not work. I asked if I could work for them for three dollars a day; I even told them I would work a whole month. The lady said they needed to sell her soon, and she thanked me for stopping by. It was a sad ride back home.

I had one more ace to play: our landlord, Mr. Dewitt Crawford.

The next Sunday afternoon I rode my bicycle up to have a visit with Mr. Dewitt. This was in the hot months of summer in the heart of Dixie. The Crawfords lived not very far from the high school, about a two-and-a-half-mile ride from our house to their house. So far I had not said anything to my parents about this blind horse. It was a very hot day as I parked my bicycle in their front yard. In the past when I needed money to buy something, Mr. Dewitt would find something for me to do. I had my fingers crossed as I knocked on their front door. His wife, Mrs. Ann, came to see what I wanted. I asked her if Mr. Dewitt was home, and if he was, could I come in and talk to him. She said, "Yes, he is." Then she said, "Wipe your feet" (I was barefoot) and invited me in. I think she was surprised to see me there on a Sunday afternoon.

We had a really good talk; he talked to me about how much care blind horses needed. He was a very practical man, always had been. He said twenty-five dollars was a lot of money to pay for a blind horse. He told me how much work it would be and all the potential problems that could come up. He knew how much work I was doing already, and that our family had no money. He also knew that whatever money we made had to go back into the family as a whole.

Mr. Dewitt would go way out of his way to help people, but he did not like those who spent money foolishly. I think he was thinking that this was a foolish thing. I could tell by the questions he had asked me. For sure I was not thinking about anything but trying to save that blind horse from being sold to the soap factory. Well, maybe I was a bit selfish because I wanted that horse.

Well, anyway he told me that he was not going to help me in this case. He was so right about the whole thing. Tears started to roll down my face; he left the room, and Mrs. Ann escorted me to the front door, gave me a pat on the shoulder, and told me to be careful riding back home. Yes, the tears were about my feelings; I had been turned down. I really wanted that horse, and most of all the tears were for that beautiful and wonderful animal; she was blind, yes, but she couldn't help it. I thought we all should be kind to animals and more so to a blind horse...I still think that way.

Mr. Dewitt was right. It was a very personal thing for me. Too many emotions, no money, and I was way too young to understand all that was involved with this handicapped filly. It was a long ride back home on that old bicycle. My mind was racing this way and that way. I knew my parents would not let me have something that my other siblings could not have. Well, at least I had given it a good try.

I did not want to know what happened to that beautiful animal. I was afraid to ask, afraid that she would meet her fate and that her young life would end way too soon. The horse could not help it that she was born that way and I thought she deserved a way much better life. I tried to help her.

In summary, Mr. Dewitt was a very smart man. He listened to me, he questioned me, and he reasoned with me, but most of all he made the right decision for me. He used common sense. I have always believed he had a PhD in common sense.

So many times, the right answer is "no."

Two dollars too much

I had cut sprouts in Mr. Dewitt's pasture for three days. He would check on me from time to time to make sure I was okay and to see that I was doing what he had hired me to do. Our dad had made arrangements for me to work for him for three dollars a day. It was not hard work, but it was in the middle of summer and I would have much rather been swimming in the creek in our pasture. There were lots of small trees trying to grow in his pasture, and lots of unwanted weeds trying to crowd out the grass that his cattle needed.

I was about twelve years old and by then I knew what was expected of me. I worked about four hours in the morning, took a little break at noon, and worked about four hours in the afternoon. Then I would go back home, do my chores, and then go down to the creek and go swimming/take a bath. Anyway, at the end of the third day, Mr. Dewitt paid me and told me that I did a good job. (He always checked, even on the little things.) I took the money, put it in my pocket, and started home. When I got out on the road, I took the money out of my pocket just to see it and feel it and count it again. My goodness, Mr. Dewitt had made a mistake! There were not just nine dollars; there were eleven dollars, all one-dollar bills! So, I turned around and went back to his house. He was sitting out under a shade tree as I walked up. He asked me what was wrong. I told him he paid me too much and counted it out so he could see. He took the money and then he counted it again right there in front of me. He counted it real slow so I could see what he was doing one dollar at a time; it was nine dollars, just what we had agreed on. I thought to myself, *what is going on here? I know there was two dollars too much; I counted it twice, and each time there were eleven dollars.* Mr. Dewitt folded it up, handed it back to me, and said for me to go on home. He thanked me again for doing a good job.

I left his yard with that dumb look on my face and headed home. I counted it three or four more times, and it always was eleven dollars. Two dollars too much. Mr. Dewitt was messing with my mind, in a good way. When I got home, I told my mom what had happened and showed her the eleven one-dollar bills. She smiled and said, "He just gave you a tip, something extra for doing a good job." She told me to keep the two-dollar tip and give the rest to our dad. I was beside myself! A tip? My first tip ever! I was all smiles.

Things I like about Mr. Dewitt Crawford

First of all, I thought he was a rich man, and he probably was, yet he always wore the same kind of clothes we did; most of the time it was bib overalls, a plain cotton shirt, and an old hat. He almost always had an old pipe in his mouth, and was always lighting it.

He did not talk a lot, and I was always wondering what he was thinking. Maybe I didn't want to know. He never brought bad news to us, and he always liked us because we showed up and we worked.

He never flattered us with words. It was just "good job" or a plain "thank you."

His yesses were always yes and his no's were always no.

He always told it like it was; there was no beating around the bush when he talked.

He did not like lazy people and he made no bones about that.

He always demanded that everyone be on time. If he had to wait for someone, they would hear about it in front of everyone.

When baling hay, he always drove one of the tractors and never worked any of us too hard.

He was always respectful of my mom and my sisters, and one time he asked our dad if he was not working them too hard. Yet he liked it that our whole family worked in the field.

He was as honest as any man on God's earth…always.

When working for him, you had to always earn the dollar he paid you. No free rides with him.

Mr. Dewitt Crawford was just a plain and simple man and I think most everyone who knew him liked him.

We could never have had a better landlord.

He was always so good to us.

Mr. Dewitt was alright. I won't ever forget him.

Mr. Dewitt Crawford 1950 at age 57

2
RED RADIO FLYER WAGON

December 25, 1946, was the first Christmas that I remember. We had no Christmas tree in our house, no Christmas lights, or any decorations. Christmas was just another day. We were setting around the kitchen table, Mom holding our baby sister, Fran, our grandpa and dad talking. After we finished breakfast, Mom stood up from the table, laid the baby in Grandpa's arms, left the room, and returned with the prettiest little red wagon! The little red wagon was for both Conley, who was four years old, and me. I was five. It was brand new and smelled like new. The little wagon was shiny, red, and beautiful! What a sight! We both scrambled from the table to be the first to ride, push, pull, and play with that wonderful toy. We enjoyed it immensely. I pulled while Conley rode or I pushed while he guided it around our yard.

The wagon didn't last all that long as we were having way too much fun with it. Of course, we were boys, and we had to take it apart to see how a wagon was made. About three months was its life span, and by then the wheels and the tongue were used up. It was pretty much junk.

That was the first and last "store-bought" gift that I remember receiving for Christmas, and the memory is still there today, as fresh as it was yesterday, six decades later. What a Christmas it was…the perfect gift for two little boys to share.

The refrigerator box

The refrigerator box was the largest box that I had ever seen. It was like a small house. Where did it come from? How did they get that thing into our house? We just looked at it for a while as it sat on the floor in our front room.

First we thought, *what in the world is so big that it fits into that big cardboard box? And what is a 'refrigerator'?*

Christmas morning, 1947, I was six years old. Our dad had a fire going in the stone fireplace. Mom was in the kitchen, and the smell of coffee and ham cooking on the wood-burning cook stove was making its way into the living room. Conley and I looked in amazement at that big cardboard box lying there. Our little sister, Lena Elizabeth, was now up; she gave the big box one look and crawled inside. She was sitting quietly, looking so happy and content, as if she were the queen of that cardboard house. And she was. Then we all piled in, and what a wonderful feeling it was as we had the best playhouse ever. Breakfast was soon ready, and our mom had to demand that we leave the comfort of that box and sit ourselves down at the kitchen table.   We played in that box for weeks. That plain cardboard box was the best sanctuary for all of us kids. We had so much fun! We ate inside, slept inside, and even the dog, Jack, was invited in. What wonderful memories with such a thing as a big ole cardboard box. Christmas that year was the best any of us kids could ever have dreamed about.

Cedar trees

In 1948, we moved to the hollow; it was a much larger house, a beautiful location with lots of wooded area. Hills with acres of trees just outside our front and back doors. A creek ran through our pasture and was lined with trees on both sides. During the year, as we walked, played, and explored the trails in that beautiful area, I took notice of what I called a Christmas tree. I remembered where it was and how it was shaped so that when Christmas came, I could make the best selection. When I see a beautiful cedar tree between four and ten feet tall, I still to this day think of it as a Christmas tree.

I was now seven years old and realized that other families that lived close by usually had a Christmas tree in their house; I wanted one, too. I thought that we had to have the biggest and the best tree. From time to time, I checked to make sure my selection was there and that it still looked good. About a week before Christmas, Conley and I took a crosscut saw, cut the cedar down, and dragged it into our house. It was all we could do to pull the cedar through the door and into the front room. Our parents thought the tree took up too much room, but in my mind it had to be a big tree. We spent a considerable amount of time setting it up in the corner of our living room. We found some strings and wrapped it around the tree, tacking it to the wall so that it stood straight in the corner and wouldn't fall down.

We had no decorations to put on the tree and no lights. All of us kids cut up strips of newspaper from the *Decatur Daily* and hung them on the tree, using the comic pages of the newspaper for color. Sometimes we strung popcorn, and sometimes we placed our school pictures on a string and hung them on the tree. In a few days, the cedar tree was beautiful in our country farm house there on Rural Route One. The cedar tree made the whole house smell so good.

Of course each year the tree would be a different size and shape. One year we set the tree in a feed bucket as we had been told that if we filled the bucket with water, the tree would stay greener longer. That was a good idea, except that we did not know a tiny hole was in the bottom of the bucket. Oh, well...we had a rag mop that took care of that.

Christmas was so much simpler back then. In our house, no presents were under the tree; nothing was wrapped, no gifts, and no hurrying to be the first one up on Christmas morning. We knew it was Christmas, and knew it was a special day for sure. The day was special because of what was going on in the kitchen: the smells that came from the cooking on our wood-burning stove.

Our farm house and buildings in the hollow

Cakes and pies

A few days before Christmas, our mom would bake a pineapple upside-down cake; in fact, she would bake two and make a two- and sometimes three-layer cake. The cakes came out of the oven golden brown with the brown sugar and pineapples sizzling. Mom dressed them up, poured hot pineapple juice over them, and then just let them sit. We could only look, smell, and drool. That wasn't fair! The next day Mom would bake a second cake using a real coconut. We would take a hammer and a nail, make a hole, and drain the juice out of it. The juice was saved for the cake later. The coconut was cracked, grated, and made ready. A tall four-layer cake was baked, and egg whites were beaten with a fork for icing. The juice from the coconut was mixed into the icing, and then grated coconut was spread between each layer. What a sight it was to see three or four cakes sitting there a day or so before Christmas.

Also, every Christmas a pecan pie was baked, and later, as our family increased in size, two pies were baked. All of us kids shelled the pecans and, of course, Mom kept a close eye on us as we would be eating them just about as fast as we shelled them. Then the pies were mixed together, and we all helped with the layering of pecans as they were made ready to bake in the oven of the wood-burning stove. Both pies were golden brown as they came out of the cook stove in our farmhouse.

Our kitchen was a busy place, and all of us kids were excited and couldn't wait for Christmas Day to come. The aroma was intoxicating. The worst part, and the hardest thing, was seeing the pies and cakes on the table, all looking so delicious and inviting, and yet we could not taste them until Christmas Day. All of us kids were looking at all that wonderful food and knowing that, for now, all we could do was just look. The sight of those pies and cakes sitting there was so enticing; we were only permitted to lick the pan or the mixing spoon. That was the only taste we were allowed, and we all thought it wasn't fair that we had to wait for Christmas Day.

Christmas Day

Christmas Day was always special. Of course, we had cows to milk, animals to feed, and the daily chores to do, but the day was special. After chores, Mom would make us a huge breakfast of ham, sausage, fried bologna, eggs, milk gravy, syrup from our home-grown sorghum and warmed on the stove, and, of course, biscuits that Mom made from scratch. Then between noon and three in the afternoon, we had the most wonderful dinner of fried chicken, country ham, canned vegetables from our garden, sweet potatoes, and, yes, cornbread. Usually, if Grandpa McCollum was with us, he told us kids a really good story. Later, he and our dad went into the living room and smoked while we kids helped our mom clean up the table. Then the cakes and pies were served and, believe me, they were just as delicious to taste as they were to look at. And I almost forgot. We always had a large box of peppermint candy. Christmas was for all of us the most wonderful day of the year. We all thought we were the most blessed people ever to have lived...and we were.

As an added surprise, Mr. Dewitt Crawford and his daughter, Sue, would arrive in his pick-up truck. Sue would get out and bring a large sack of oranges and a box of apples to our front door. We were so lucky and fortunate to have him as our landlord. Sue still remembers the smiles on our faces and how happy we were as she left our front porch. She said, "That was always the best part of Christmas for me as I helped Dad deliver all this to our friends on Rural Route One."

Two more days

Christmas, with the pies, cakes, peppermint candy, oranges, and apples, lasted for a few more days. It was like the best thing ever! We ate our fill of all that wonderful food. It seemed that the cakes and pies improved with each day, and for sure all of us kids wanted to savor the taste, meaning, and memories of that part of the year. The last day of the year, Conley and I were responsible for taking down that giant cedar tree and dragging it out of the house without destroying something. It was a messy job. Later, we decided that a smaller tree would serve the purpose in a much better and easier way.

This was pretty much how all our Christmases were in the 1940s and 50s. No presents. No boxes wrapped in fancy paper. No blinking lights. Yet I would not trade any of those Christmases on that rural, dirt road for anything else in the world. If we were poor, we didn't know it, and NEVER did we feel like we were ever neglected.

We always had the best Christmas ever...we were so blessed: we had a home, plenty of food, a wonderful family, and the best neighbors.

3

"THE CRIPPLE BOY"

The school bus driver would save the seat just behind him for the cripple boy. In fact, that was the only place he could set. His one leg was in iron braces and he could not bend it. He used crutches to get around and, for the most part, he did very well. He did not need any help; in fact, he got disgusted when someone tried to give him a hand.

I liked this little guy. I think he was about two years younger than me. But what a neat kid he was. At that time, I took everything for granted. I could run, play softball and basketball, swim, and do just about anything I wanted to. I did not realize how blessed I was.

He lived up the road from us close to Hebron Church. He had a wonderful family; they lived in a plain but very nice house. He always looked nice, had on clean clothes, his hair was always combed, and he was so easy to talk to. He was so smart and so very interested in everything, it seemed.

Someone told me that he had polio and that if you touched him you could get it and then you would be crippled also. I had to think about that for a while, but thought that was crazy. Polio was new to me; I had not heard much about that back in the early 1950s. I would set behind him and we would talk. Later he asked me to come sit with him as we could talk better. I did not have to think twice; I moved up one seat and we talked about everything from shooting marbles to homemade flip stocks, at which he was an expert.

He had the best parents and they loved him so much; it was so obvious. They took very good care of him, yet he was not spoiled. He had chores to do just like his siblings. Just because he wore braces on one leg he did not have it any easier than anyone else. He was an excellent student; he would read something to me while riding home on the bus that he thought was profound. I was impressed and he knew I was impressed. He was kind of funny also. He told me one time that he was better off than I was and that he had it made...I was thinking, *how?* He said because of his braces he did not have to pick cotton. He most surely had a point there.

I think most of the other students did not pay much attention to him and, for the most part, he blended in with all of us. One time he told me about an older kid who was making fun of him and had called him a "polio boy" and that made him mad. He said he walked right up to the bully, turned, and with the leg that had the braces on, struck the bully in the ankle and darn near broke the other kid's leg. Later he had to go talk to his teacher. He said the other kid was punished and he got a pat on the back. He had powerful shoulders and arms and could outdo anyone at arm wrestling. He definitely could take care of himself. I liked that about him.

He had the best attitude and I do not think he thought anything other than he was a blessed kid. I learned so much from him by just talking and setting there on the seat with him. One time he asked me what I knew about honey bees. I said, "Well, I know they will sting you." We both laughed and then he told me the most wonderful story about the life and works of the honey bee. He gave me a pamphlet about all that. I still have that today.

Over the years I have always wished that I would have kept in touch with him. He made such an impression on me that have lasted all my life. I remember his positive attitude, his easygoing nature. I do not think he ever thought he was any different than the rest of us boys. For sure he did not think he was disable; he just had to go about things a bit different than the rest of us. He was one of the good guys…and my friend.

Here, I am sad to say that I am not sure that I remember his name. I think his last name was Mitchell.

I do not know what happened to him; his family moved and the seat there on the bus was vacant. It was a sad time for me for a few days. I really missed him, my school bus buddy.

4

MR. DENSMORE'S
WATERMELON PATCH

On Rural Route One, there were fields of corn, cotton, hay, sorghum, and peanuts alongside the country dirt roads. It was a sight to see as all the farmers planted and harvested their crops. They took a lot of pride in how straight their rows were and how clean they kept their fields. For it was a known fact that it would be mentioned at the Hulaco General Store. If it looked bad, it would reflect on your ability as a farmer. If your rows were crooked, someone would say, "Was the wind blowing when you planted that corn?" Then the farmer with the crooked rows would say, "No…but you know you harvest more corn from crooked rows."

Everything was there in plain sight for all to see and for sure every farmer looked at his neighbor's crop all year long as they passed by. AND they still do today. But there are some crops that you do not plant along the side of a country road. No, sirree, one of them would be watermelons. The watermelon patch would be hid behind the corn, or in the middle of the field, or across the road from the farm house behind the Kentucky wonder pole beans.

Mr. and Mrs. Densmore, two of the nicest people you would ever want to meet, lived in a very scenic area along that country road on Rural Route One. Mr. Densmore was a good farmer who took pride in his home, farm, and his wonderful family. All the Densmores were like that. They were great neighbors and fun people…all of them.

I grew up with some really nice neighbor kids all about my age. One of them was Larry. Larry was full of life and always a happy go lucky kind of a kid. He was a go-getter, easy to get along with, and full of ideas. He was a bit mischievous in a good way. We were now about twelve years old—almost teenagers—and we had more energy than you would ever believe. Larry was telling me one time that Mr. Densmore had the best watermelons ever and he had so many different kinds: Dixie queen, sweet beauty, and yellow orange sweet. I forgot to ask him how he knew all that…maybe I didn't need to know.

I am not sure when the statute of limitations ends for taking a watermelon that is not yours. I hope after sixty-plus years I am in the clear. August in Northern Alabama can be a very hot month, sometimes well over a hundred degrees. A cool watermelon is so tasty on a hot summer afternoon. Larry and I were just hanging out as it was way too hot to be doing anything else. Two idle minds sitting there on the creek bank. And as you know, the devil loves idle minds. Yep, it was the devil. That's who I can blame all this on. It was the devil's fault.

We were thinking how good a cool watermelon would taste. It was so darn hot on this Sunday afternoon. Yes, it was the Lord's Day. If we just had a good melon we could let it sit in the creek and the water would cool it down and what a treat that would be. I looked at Larry and he looked at me and our minds came together thinking about the same thing. See how two minds are much better than one? Yeah, right. Mr. Densmore's watermelon patch…it was as clear as mud. We headed up the hill through the trees and bushes to the crime scene. Now as we made our way through the woods, all at once I had a funny feeling inside me. It was more like a scary feeling. I now had second thoughts about all this but was thinking that I could not back out now. I didn't want to be called "chicken." That was the worst thing ever to be called when you are twelve years old.

We made it through the woods to the top of the hill and there was the corn field. I waited there in the woods; Larry went to find just the right one, as he knew his melons better than I did. It seemed like I had waited for hours. Then there he came with a really nice-size one. We made a bee line back down through the woods to the creek. About halfway there I had to tote it for a while…that thing was heavy. Now back to the creek and the cool running water. We were both thinking how long it would take to cool it down; we did not want to wait too long. About an hour later, we couldn't wait any longer. On a large, flat rock we busted it and what a sight it was. It was a "sweet yellow one" and, boy, was it ever good. We ate the whole thing. Larry headed home and I went to our barn to do the evening chores.

About a half-hour into the chores I was not feeling so good. In fact, I was getting sick. I mean up-chucking sick. What was wrong with me? Now I was thinking that I had taken part in a crime on the Lord's Day…what had I done? About ten minutes later I made it to the house and into the kitchen, where my mom was fixing supper. She looked at me and said, "What is wrong with you?" I said I was sick. From here on, it was not going to be one of my better days…. not by a long shot.

She started asking me all kinds of questions…moms are like that, you know. Anyway, she wanted to know why I was sick. I didn't know. "What have you eaten?" Why would she ask me that? Was part of the evidence on my face? I said, "Some watermelon." She asked, "Where did you get the watermelon?" I said, "From Larry." She was now very close to my face. "Where did Larry get it?" she said in a much different and stronger tone. I said, without thinking that I was lying to dear Mother…I said with the most innocent look that I could muster at this critical point in my young life…I said, "I don't know." Right at this point in this one-sided conversation, my sweet, easygoing mom, who hardly ever said more than just a few words, turned into a crime-scene investigator. I had never seen her like this before. Now I was scared, even though I was a good-size kid and a bit taller than her. I was now just about as strong as Jell-O and was shaking like it, too. She grabbed me by my t-shirt and turned me around and backed me up to the wood-burning cook stove, so close that my rear end was now also feeling the heat, but nothing like what I felt inside. She said, "You don't know?" I was now sick in a very different way…I was really sick now. My red-headed mom was upset with me—no, she was red-faced MAD, I mean mad! She still had me in a chokehold with that t-shirt very tight around my neck.

Confession is good for the soul, they say. I had no choice…well, that or death from choking.

Now all my brothers and sisters were bystanders listening to all the commotion in our kitchen. My mom was now going crazy. She turned me around and introduced me as a "thief" living there among them. "A thief?" I said. "I am not a thief"…I said that to myself as by now I dared not even open my mouth. She was announcing to everyone what I had done and what a pitiful sight I was. She was talking non-stop, bad-mouthing me in the very worst way ever. She had never before done anything like that. This was my dear mom, the mom that would fight for me and even give her life for me. I now was being bad-mouthed there in front of all my brothers and sisters as a condemned thief. She was the judge and the jury, and it was appearing that if I lived through this, she would be the warden. I looked over at my brother, Conley, and I thought I saw a slight grin on his face, and my sister, Fran, had that look that said, "He deserves to be taken out back and shot!" All I did was eat a little watermelon. Gosh.

She sat me down in a chair—maybe I should say she forced me down—and was now towering over me and then reached for the Good Book. She opened it to Exodus chapter 20, handed it to me, and made me read it out loud so everyone could hear—verse 15: "Thou Shalt Not Steal"—as my squeaky voice trembled. Then she and everyone just looked at me…all of them just setting and standing there looking at me. You could have heard a pin drop. I could smell the corn bread cooking in that wood-burning stove in our kitchen and was hoping that she would go take care of that. For sure I was hoping that the burning cornbread in the oven would save me…but no. Now I was a condemned kid at only twelve years old. Going to hell, for sure. I wanted so badly to read verse 13 to her, "Thou Shall Not Kill," but I didn't want to give her any ideas. By now I was not sick from the watermelon anymore. It was a much worse kind of sickness!

Things really went downhill from here, as if it could have gotten worse. She told my dad to watch the cook stove and she grabbed me by the shirt, pulled me to my feet, and said we are going for a walk. I was thinking and hoping that we did not have a rope strong enough to hang me with. No, in a way this was much worse than hanging. She marched me about a mile up the road to Mr. Densmore's house. She walked up on their porch as if she were the high sheriff, knocked loudly on the front door, and announced that she had a boy who is a thief and needed to confess his sins to them. They came out and sat down then my mom left me standing there in front of the firing squad. My life as I knew it was over…I mean over!

They told me to sit down and tell them why I was there. I had to tell them the truth 'cause if I didn't, my mom would have. Well, I don't know what she would have done to me if I would have lied. I told them the whole story…the whole story. Told them it was my fault and tried not to blame it on Larry, even though it was his idea. (Yeah, right, as if that would have helped my case.) The Densmores just talked to me. They were not mad; in fact, I think they were feeling kinda sorry for me. And I mean sorry in the right way.

Anyway, they forgave me and said that if I ever wanted a watermelon, just stop by and they would go with me out to the patch and help me find just the right one. I got the message. Mrs. Densmore gave me a hug. Mr. Densmore walked me out to the road and told me a short story about a similar time in his life when he was my age; that made me feel much better. We shook hands and he invited me to stop and visit when I wanted to. WOW, what a great feeling. It is so good to be forgiven…sooooooo good.

Now it was almost dark and I hoofed it back home thinking maybe I would be sleeping in the barn for the rest of my life. The big brother of the clan was now branded as a thief.

For the next year or so, I was the best kid ever…I mean ever! I was the best big brother anyone could ever hope to have. I had learned a very valuable lesson. I think my mom forgave me; the worst thing ever is to lose someone's trust. I will never, even if I live to be a hundred years old, ever forget about that Sunday afternoon and Mr. Densmore's watermelon patch. Nor will I ever forget how disappointed my mom was with me. Of all the people in the world, your mom is one you can always turn to when you are in trouble, but only if you are not a watermelon thief.

5

SWIMMING WITH THE SNAKES

I saw something moving in the water, and I stood there in my birthday suit watching and wondering what it could be. I asked Cicero, who was getting undressed and ready to jump in, what that was in the water. He came over and looked and said, "It looks like a water moccasin." I was thinking, whoa. He said, "Ah, don't worry." About that time, here came Hugo and he jumped in and made a big splash; water went everywhere. I wondered where that snake went.

This was the summer of 1953 and I was well into my twelfth year of life. I had been swimming in this water hole for three or four years; in fact, all of us local kids had so much fun swimming in this small creek. It was called the Price Hole. Just a little creek that ran through a wooded area not far from where we lived in the hollow. The best way to get there was to walk about a half-mile on the dirt road up the hill to the Ellenburgs' place then walk down through their pasture and back down a hill with trees and bushes all around. This was the best place ever to go swimming.

This little creek was about five or six feet deep in the middle and is where I learned how to swim, or maybe I didn't have a choice. A few years back, I was wading in the shallow part of this creek, taking a bath, washing myself with a bar of Lifebuoy soap. I was just having a good ole time when Pete and Billy Wayne grabbed me, one on each side, and tossed me in. I went under and hit bottom and bounced back up, and with my mouth full of creek water. Then I dog-paddled my way out. Up until this time I had not gone out into the deeper part. I just waded out and then back to safety. Pete, my buddy, said I needed to learn how to swim. I said, "I will one of these days when I get good and ready." He said, "Today is the day and you better be ready" and they threw me in.

Now as I watched Hugo swim around—and then Pete, Larry, and Cicero jumped in—I was thinking, *they are swimming with the snakes.* Now, I was not the kind of kid who, if everyone jumped off a cliff, I would follow. Not by a long shot. But I had washed and bathed in this creek for the past few years. So I said, *what the heck?* I backed up, made a run for it, and dove in. I came back up quickly and could see small holes in the creek bank on both sides and was hoping that the water moccasin had made it into one of those holes. Up until then I had not paid much attention to the small holes in the banks… now I was looking to see if there was anything looking back at me. For the most part, I was not all that scared of snakes. There were all kinds of them living around us: rattlesnakes, diamond backs, and, of course, the water moccasin.

This was the only creek that ran close to where I lived that was deep enough to dive into. Most of the time we all went together as I did not want to go swimming by myself. We had fun in this creek as we played king of the mountain, trying to see who could throw everyone in and then the last one left standing would be the king. At times we would get scratched up and a couple of times some of us got hurt. We would gang up on the bigger and older guys and try to throw them in first. The banks would be wet and sometimes we all went in together.

One time, Mr. John Ellensburg happened to come down and catch us horsing around and he thought we had better stop as it looked like we were having way too much fun. He said for us to stop that as someone might get hurt. Of course we stopped but it was not much fun just diving in and then back out. A week or so later we were all there and again we started seeing who we could throw in, just horsing around. Larry, Hilton, Cicero, and me. We were having a good ole time as we were trying to throw Cicero in. We all slipped and Cicero ended up on the bottom as we all fell in and, my goodness, as we were climbing back out and onto the bank, Cicero said his arm was really hurting. We all stopped, got dressed, and made sure Cicero got back home. Later we found out that his arm was broken. Mr. John was looking right at me and was very upset as he knew that I most likely was the cause of his son's broken arm. Cicero had a cast on for over a month and his dad was still mad at me because it cost him thirty dollars to get it set. I was thinking he was probably going to give me a good whopping but I lucked out!

Now that I knew there were snakes living in that swimming hole, I was a bit more careful. Before we jumped in, we would find a good-sized rock and throw it in and that would scare the snakes away. The snakes would head for a hole in the bank. After a while we did not pay much attention to them. But swimming with the snakes was always a worry and it took away from the fun for a while.

One time, Billy Wayne told me not to worry too much about them snakes as they were more afraid of us than we were of them. I was thinking, *I am not so sure about that.* I thought that I would test his story as I had found a real look-alike toy rubber snake…it looked so real. The next time we were there, I would see if his theory was going to work. We all got undressed, threw a rock in, and all of us dove in and were swimming around and just having a good ole time. I went over while Billy Wayne was in the water and I laid that rubber snake just under his britches. Later I watched as he was ready to go and getting dressed. He saw that toy snake and he just about went crazy. He found a limb and was beating that toy snake to pieces. We all laughed until our sides hurt. He grabbed me and threw me in the water then he jumped in and for a while I was thinking that he was going to drown me.

We always had so much fun at the Price Hole, just a mountain stream that turned into a creek out in the middle of the woods. We usually did not have much time to go swimming, but, when we did, it served two purposes. One, we really enjoyed getting cooled off on a hot summer day and, two; we had the best bath ever. All of us in our birthday suits.

Now thinking back, it gives me the shivers thinking about how poisonous those snakes were. The water moccasin is one of the most poisonous. The rattlesnake most always warns you that it is going to strike. I often wondered if the others just sneak up behind you and bite you on the butt. I think we all lucked out. I can just imagine a swimming pool in the city and seeing a snake there; I think the police force would be called out and the pool closed for the day.

Swimming with the snakes was, to say the least, very exciting!

6

ONE ROW AT A TIME

The rows were straight, about thirty-eight inches wide, and just about as uniform as they could be. All of our corn and cotton was planted with a one-row planter. One row at a time. It seemed that the mule knew just where to walk. We would plant about fifteen acres of cotton and fifteen acres of corn using this method. Back in the late 1940s and '50s, I do not know how many years we were behind the more modern farmers who lived in other states; it had to be at least a decade, maybe more. It was a slow process but we made it work. It took us about three days to plant fifteen acres.

For me it was exciting getting everything ready to plant. By then the fields had been plowed, disked, and dragged. Now to get the seed and the printed fertilizer sacks loaded on the wagon. We would set the fertilizer and seed sacks on the ground along the end of the field, just about where they might be needed. My grandpa was good at estimating where each sack should be placed. Then back to the barn to load the fertilizer distributer and the planter on the wagon. We only had two mules. This would take at least a good hour to get everything ready to plant.

One mule was harnessed to the distributer then the hopper filled with fertilizer. My grandpa would then go up to the mule and rub her nose and ears while he talked to her, like he was saying that we have to work as a team, "You do your part and I will do my part." I thought that was so cool. He would make a couple of rounds then he gave the signal to get started. I was excited.

As I walked behind the planter and the mule, I could see each seed come out of the hopper and drop down into the shut then into the furrow and the side sweeps would pull the soil over the seed and the rear packing wheel firmed the soil. I was amazed at this simple farm tool, how it worked, and even at that early age I knew that the planter was the most important implement on the farm.

Now this might appear to you, the reader, as a pretty simple task. It was so much more than just following that old mule. First of all, I was nine years old. My picture on the front cover of this book was taken when I was nine years old.

To get our crops planted one row at a time, most everything had to work in unison, just like today but on a so much smaller scale. The mule had to do its part and she did. She was slow, did not get excited, and knew what was expected of her. She had to walk straight, know when to stop, and know which way to turn at the end of the row. We most always had pretty good mules. The planter had to be in good working order, and that was my job. A few days before we started this operation, I would make sure it was greased and all the moving parts were in good shape. I had to keep the planter upright, which was not an easy job at that young age. I had to know about how many rows one hopper full would plant. The mule and I had to know how to communicate to each other. We both needed to know "gee" from "haw." If I gave the wrong command, the mule would get confused; then we had to stop and start all over again (kinda like a drill sergeant marching his troops). At the end of the rows, the mule and I had to get turned around without turning the planter over and dumping the seeds out on the ground. The planter full of seed weighed much more than I did.

Being in charge of the planting starting at about nine years old and for the next seven years was one of the most important jobs on our farm. I had to do it right. There was no room for error. I felt like I was an important part of this farm operation—and I was. When the corn and cotton started to grow, I could see how good of a job the mule and I did with how straight the rows were…and of course the neighbors who went by would always look to see how our crops looked. They still do that today. We planted one row at a time, hoed one row at a time, cultivated one row at a time, and harvested one row at a time.

Just a few months back, I watched one of my farmer friends plant his corn with a twenty-four-row planter. The big, green, four-hundred-horse-power tractor was moving across the field at a pretty good speed…around five miles an hour. Twenty-four rows at a time…WOW. He had a GPS system in the cab of his air-conditioned tractor. The planter and the tractor were a complicated state-of-the-art system that made sure each seed was placed at the right space. The monitor in the cab of his tractor kept track of all twenty-four rows and seed population, and, at a moment's notice, would let him know if something went wrong.

Gosh, when I was planting corn, I was the monitor and the mule was the GPS. The mule knew where to go, how to get there, and at just the right speed.

Today my farmer friend farms a little over two thousand acres and he helps feed the world. He is so much more than just a farmer and so much more educated. What would we do without the American farmer?

One row at a time versus twenty-four rows. I choose twenty-four rows.

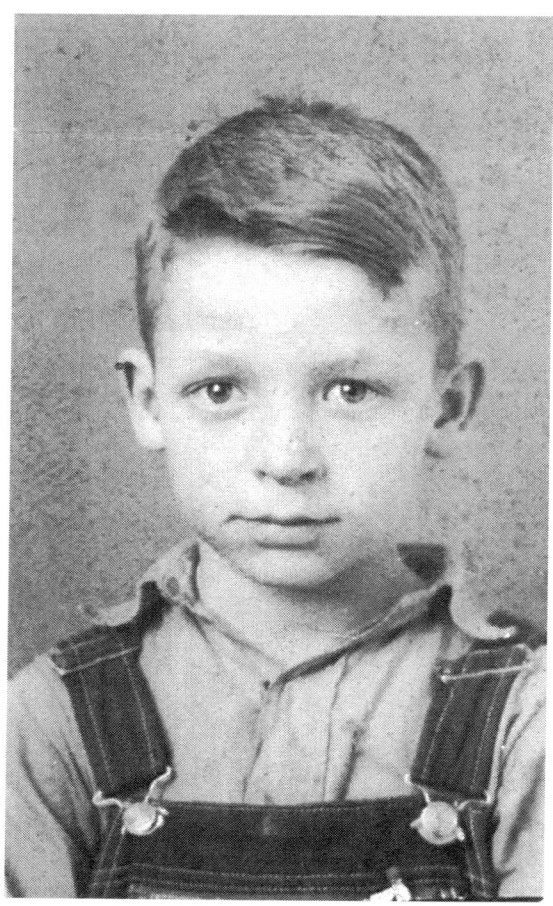

Little Will age nine

7

HOG-KILLING TIME

Those two pigs were hungry; they were always hungry. Yes, I know they were animals, just pigs, but these two seemed to have a personality…call it pig personality or something. They knew we were taking good care of them.

We usually had two or three hogs on our farm. There was a slop bucket in our kitchen where Mom threw all the scraps that were left over from the table. We took this and gave to the hogs each day. The hogs really liked this; as they saw you coming, you had better get it emptied into the trough or they would knock you down trying to get to the bucket. I think for the most part, with all of us hungry kids, the scraps were few. The pigs were also fed corn and a mixture of other types of feed. I remember the hogs just roaming around for a while in the pasture and in the yard, and then sometimes they were in a pen. We most of the time made pets out of the farm animals, all except the chickens (I guess if we only had two or three, they would have been pets also). The pigs would lie down and want us to rub their bellies; we were their friends and they did not think we would ever hurt them. At least that is what I think they thought.

In the fall, as the weather started to get really cold, it was hog-killing time. Our friends and neighbors would come over to get this thing started. Also, I believe there were people who lived nearby who did this a lot, helping other farmers kill hogs just for the meat, and they were good at doing this sort of thing. I remember some of our neighbors doing this; it was a big deal to them, like having a Southern-style all-day cook out. I believe most of them looked forward to this. For them it was a really fun thing. I guess getting everyone together, laughing, talking, cutting up that pig, and having a big dinner with all that fresh meat was a big to do thing.

I know a lot of people who were born in the wrong time; they should have been born a hundred years earlier. They love to hunt, trap, and eat meat. They are hunters, and would have been right at home living back in those times, hunting buffalo, elk and deer. (My brother John is like that; He loves to hunt). They were good at that then; they had to be. Me, I would have had to find something else to eat. I was not good at that sort of thing. Cold not stand to kill or skin a rabbit or squirrel, did not like to eat them.

Never in a hundred years could I kill them.

Hog-killing day was not a good day for me. I was only at this one and never again was I home for this event. It made me sick or even more than sick, for it haunted me for a long time.

There was lots of work that had to be completed in a short amount of time. First of all, someone had to come over with a rifle to do that job. The hogs would be enticed to come to a certain area, usually close to the old walnut tree at the edge of the field out back, usually with the slop bucket. As for me, I thought that was cruel.

But this was nothing compared to what happened later. I won't go into details, but I could not stand this. One time was enough for me as I completely lost it when I saw what had happened to them pigs.

I wondered what they were thinking—if pigs think, and I think they do. The pigs by this time would be in a pen and my dad would open the gate and entice them out with the slop bucket. Both would look at him and come a-running. They thought, *hey, this is something! We are getting food this early in the morning…this is going to be a good day.* Yeah, right. *The fellow who scratches our ears is here; it must be safe even if there are a few strangers standing around looking. But why are we being fed at the walnut tree? Wonder what that hot water in that pot is for…this is not wash day. Hey, where is the slop?* Then bang, bang. (I know…I know…but this is what happened.)

I ran from this scene. For a while I was a mess. My dad then told me to go do something else and excused me from taking part in this ugly thing. I do not want to go on about all this as it is something that I wish I had never witnessed. The smell was not good. (If it doesn't smell good, I don't go there.) The killing area around that walnut tree was a sight that I do not ever want to see again. It was sickening. The meat was cut and prepared, lard was made, and the crackling stored later to make crackling bread. The meat was salted down and stored in the back room of our house.

Our kitchen was turned into a processing center: sausage was ground, the hogs cut and sliced, and meat was everywhere. Everyone had something to do and it looked like everyone was having a good ole time. The smell was sickening to me; even for weeks afterwards, it seemed like I could still smell that smell.

The folks that helped us were given part of the meat for their help. Pretty much all of the hog was used and/or given away. We did not make chittlins or use the head; that would have really freaked me out.

These were farm animals, part of life there on the farm. We always took care of them and they all knew we cared for them. I did not want to eat the meat or even touch it. Of course everyone thought that I was weird…and maybe I am.

Hog-killing time was not a good time in my life. I either had someplace to go or this was done while I was at school or had other chores to do. I am so thankful that I do not have to work in a plant where all this takes place. I do not like seeing a semi-truck hauling them to their demise. I am not a vegetarian but I eat very little meat and hardly any pork.

Hog-killing time was a big day back then for most folks; it was their food supply. Here I must say that I think it was a much better way of doing things than the way it is today. It was done in a humane way and I like that. Maybe if we would have had a hundred or more pigs and not just two, I might have felt different…I don't know.

For a long time I did not want to go near that tree where all this had taken place. Yet I knew this was the way things were. This was a part of the food supply and still is. But I don't know if I would have survived living back when you had to hunt and kill most everything you need to live on.

8

GRANNY VINES

She said, "William, let me show you how to start this car." I watched as she leaned over with a flashlight and a screwdriver; she looked under the dash, found two wires, unscrewed the nuts, and then twisted the two wires together. She set back up, opened her door, leaned over, and spit then looked at me and said, "Let's go fishing." I touched the wires to a medal bolt. The car started and we drove away, me driving a stolen car. I had just turned fourteen years old and did not have a driver's license.

Her name was Lena Leota Vines. She had some Choctaw Indian blood in her, how much I do not know. Her middle name, Leota, was given to her by an Indian chief, so we were told. I grew up thinking she was the most wonderful grandma anyone could ever have. She always looked like a granny, even when I was just a kid of five or six years old. She looked old, she acted old, she dressed old, her hair was done up in a bun on the top of her head, making her look old. She only had two or three teeth and she most always had a pinch of snuff and a sweet gum twig in her mouth. She would take the sweet gum twig and stick it into a can of snuff and then put it in her mouth. Yes, I know this sounds a bit gross but that was my granny Vines.

She was my mom's mother. My mom was as meek as a lamb, so easygoing most of the time. My granny Vines was a she-bear. She was a bit gruff, never one to mince words; you either liked her or you didn't and she didn't care much either way. She had worked all her life at whatever job she could find, from hoeing or picking cotton to cleaning and washing for other folks. Back then you had to work or you didn't eat. She was a tough lady and I liked that about her. She raised seven kids mostly by herself.

Her oldest son was my uncle Jessie. He and his wife, Aunt Irene, lived in Decatur, Alabama. They both worked at the cotton mill, both on the day shift, and they both rode the city bus to and from work. Granny Vines was living with them when I was in my teens. She had her own little apartment in one side of their house.

I ran away from home and hitchhiked to Decatur. I had planned on joining the army but was turned down because of my age. I knew I had to go back home, but I stopped to see Granny Vines and spend a day or so with her. The first morning after we got up and were having a bite to eat out on the front porch, she looked at me with a smile and said, "Let's go fishing today." I thought that was a great idea. She said we could take Jessie's car. I was thinking, *well, okay*. He owned an old 1938 Chevrolet, four-door black sedan. Uncle Jessie had won this old car with four aces in a card game. This was in 1955; it was an old car. It was older than me by three years.

She found her cane fishing poles, stuck them through the back window of the car, and brought a wooden box for her to set on with a cushion. With a happy look on her face, we were ready to roll. Granny found a small rock and left it just where the right front tire was out there on the street, up against the curb. She told me to make sure we parked it in the exact same spot so that Jessie would not know it had been moved. We were now ready to go. The old car was running pretty good, the fishing poles sticking out the window, Granny with a smiley look on her face as we drove down a side street to a little store at the edge of town. She went inside and bought fishing worms, a couple of RC Colas, some Vienna sausages, crackers, and two moon pies. I was thinking this was fishing at its very best. We had all the stuff in a paper sack, the worms in a tin can, and off we drove to the Tennessee River back waters. I had all day to just hang out with my granny. I was thinking, *I don't ever want to go back home; this is the good life.*

Granny loved to fish. She would stop what she was doing in a minute if someone said something about going fishing; she would grab her fishing pole and stay out on the river banks as long as she could. When someone came to see her, after about ten minutes into the conversation, she would say with a toothless smile, "You wanna go fishing?" She took all her kids fishing and most of her grandkids at least one time. I do not remember her ever bringing the fish she caught home with her; she always threw them back in. I liked that.

We made it out to her favorite fishing spot then she had me drive the car as far away from the road as I could, hoping that it would not be noticed by any of Uncle Jessie's friends. She had her favorite fishing pole, her favorite box to set on—it was like a ritual as everything had to be just right. We walked out along the river bank with all our stuff to the place she always fished at, and there we met one of her fishing pals. She was an older black lady about the same age as Granny. They had the best time talking and both would say something funny and both would laugh out loud. When the red and white bobber went under, they both got excited. One would say to the other, "You got a bite." I asked them how in the world they were going to catch any fish if they were always talking and laughing so loud. They both told me to just shut up and then laughed at me. I was fishing with Granny on one side and Ms. Mollie on the other side. Ms. Mollie said something about using my moon pie for bait. I looked at her, smiled, and said, "No way." Ms. Mollie said, "Then give me a bite." I laughed. She was still looking at me, so I got the moon pie out of the sack and let her have a bite. She consumed half of it with one bite. I was lucky to get the other half back…and my fingers. She said, "Thank ya" then after about a minute or two she said "You're a good boy."

Anyway, about two in the afternoon we had to head back so that we could get the car parked in the same parking spot there on the street in front of their house before Uncle Jessie got back home. We loaded everything back in the old car, said goodbye to Ms. Mollie, and away we went. Granny had me stop at a little gas station and we put a dollar's worth of gas in the tank and also dumped all our trash (getting rid of the evidence). We were driving along just fine and were about halfway back, and then all at once the car just died. I coasted off to the side of the road and was wondering what was wrong. Granny looked under the dash and said that the wires came undone. She was a bit upset with me that I did not do a better job of twisting them together. Back on the road again, I asked her, "What would happen if the cops stopped us and found out we stole Uncle Jessie's car?" She looked at me and said, "We?" She then said, "You're the one driving." I said, "I thought we were in this together" and she said, "We are...until YOU get caught." I think she was kidding me.

We made it back to the house just fine and as we turned down the block where the house was, there was another car parked in the spot where we needed to park. Granny got excited as we drove up slowly right behind the other car. She said, "We gotta move that car out of the way." She got out and walked around the other car a couple of times, I think to see if anyone was watching us. She said for me to look and see if it was a standard shift. I looked and said, "Yes, it is." I opened the door, put the shift lever in neutral, and we both pushed it about twenty feet down the street. Granny found the small rock and stood there; I drove Uncle Jessie's car up until she motioned for me to stop. Now we were home safe and Granny was looking for her snuff can. She was a happy lady. I used the screwdriver and connected the wires back to the terminals, cleaned everything up, and closed the door. She double-checked to make sure everything was just the way we found it.

Each time I went to visit her, I had to take her fishing and we always "borrowed" Uncle Jessie's car...that was her word. Going fishing in that old Chevrolet was our secret. She and I always had fun together. I think she liked me.

One last note: Uncle Jessie would from time to time tell others about the great gas mileage he was getting with his 1938 Chevrolet. It always put a big ole smile on my face when he bragged about that. I do not think he ever knew.

Lena Leota Vines

Born May 18, 1884

Died Jan. 26, 1969

9

A SILVER STAR

He was standing straight as a board in the hallway of our small country school. He looked like he was at least six feet, six inches tall in his military uniform and was picture-perfect, as if he had just stepped out of a Hollywood movie screen, talking to our principal, Mr. Randolph Ryan. He looked like a movie star. This was a first for me at Ryan High School in Morgan County, Alabama. The very first time I had seen a soldier in uniform.

Of course, all of us were in awe of this army paratrooper. His uniform fit him like a glove; his jump boots were spit-shined to a high gloss. He had silver jump wings and medals on his chest and corporal stripes on his sleeves. He was without a doubt the center of attention back in 1954. As a young teenager I wanted to grow up and be just like him.

The older students were calling him "Junior." He stayed for a while talking to everyone who came by. I wanted so much to ask him a hundred questions as I shook his hand. I wanted to get to know who he was and let him know what a great impression he made on me. But it was not to be, as a very pretty lady by the name of Virginia came by, and they walked away and out of the school building holding hands...WOW.

Little did I know then that our paths would cross a number of times over the next sixty years, and maybe at times we came face to face without knowing who each other was. Now as I sit across the table asking him so many questions, he is reluctant to answer, as I have already addressed him as a hero: a real live hero who grew up down the road from where I lived on Rural Route One, hoeing and picking cotton—a farm kid who wanted so much more out of life.

Over the years I have written so many short stories about our American veterans who, when I first talked to them, stated that, no matter what, they were not heroes. Arvin is no exception as he does not see himself that way...only as someone who did what he had to do. His military records tell a different story. He is most surely one of our heroes. Most veterans just say that what they did was what anyone would have done in the heat of battle. Yet I know it takes a special person to stand up when the bullets are coming at you and take charge as the leader; very few people have what it takes to do that.

It always impresses me to read about Alvin York and Audie Murphy and others who were just plain country kids who came back from war as heroes...just poor farm kids who did their job well, who gave their very best, and they, too, did not think they were anyone special. I believe most of our highly decorated veterans think that way. Knowing and reading about them makes me stand a bit taller and more so that Arvin Briscoe Jr. was my neighbor back in the 1940s and 50s on Rural Route One.

This story, in my opinion, should be a book, as this man has given so much of himself, has trained so hard, has endured so much, and went above and beyond the call of duty while serving his country.

The Silver Star was awarded to Sergeant First Class Arvin M. Briscoe Jr. while serving as a member of the United States Army 5th Special Forces Group in the Republic of Viet Nam. Sergeant First Class Briscoe distinguished himself through extraordinary heroism involving actions against an enemy of the United States.

Only two medals rank higher than the Silver Star: the Congressional Medal of Honor and the Distinguished Service Cross. You can see here why I and others see Arvin Briscoe as a hero, a gentleman still so full of life—and what a really wonderful person he is.

Junior grew up on a small farm just a bit east of Ryan Cross Roads, Morgan County, Alabama. At the age of sixteen, he hitchhiked to

Texas and worked in the oil fields for a few months then hitchhiked back home. In 1952, just after he turned seventeen, he and his dad made a trip to Huntsville to see the army recruiter. In the office was a large picture of an airborne soldier. "Gosh," he said. "Boy, does the guy in the picture ever look sharp." *That is for me*, he thought. *That is what I want to sign up for*—and more so when the recruiter said his pay would be an extra fifty dollars. Arvin said to himself, *It looks like I am going to be a rich man.*

While flying to Fort Jackson, South Carolina, in a DC-3 twin-engine airplane, he was amazed as he looked out the window at how far it was down. He had second thoughts about jumping from a perfectly good airplane. He was thinking that never in a hundred years would he have the nerve to strap on a parachute, stand in line, and leap out…no way. He thought to himself, *when I report in at Fort Jackson, I will tell the army that I changed my mind about the airborne thing; the extra money is not worth it.*

Arriving at Fort Jackson for basic training, he was very busy from the time the airplane landed until the end of his training. He had completely forgotten about jump school. The sixteen weeks of basic training was a piece of cake—always is for most farm kids. On graduation day, two hundred and forty-four men were standing in formation as the captain and the first sergeant were congratulating all of them upon completion of their training. Then the first sergeant called everyone to attention. He called Private Briscoe to the front and announced that he was one of the few who had what it took to become an airborne trooper; he was going to Fort Benning, Georgia, for jump school. Arvin thought, *Oh, my goodness, I forgot all about telling them that I changed my mind.* But now, standing out front with the captain and first sergeant and all eyes looking at him, he did not have the guts to back out…and the rest is history.

Basic training was a challenge but nothing compared to the training that he had to go through at the airborne training center at Fort Benning, Georgia. This was the real thing: get it right the first time; there are no second chances. There was no marching there; it was double-time, running everywhere you went. Double-time to class, double-time to the mess hall, double-time to the jump tower and to the airplane with all that weight (about sixty pounds) strapped on your back. This was special, a special unit, and Arvin could not believe that he really liked this. His thinking was, *if you are going to be a soldier, why not be one of the best?* I like his way of thinking.

This was airborne: it was tough, it was very professional, and it took a special person to make it through the four weeks of training. The dropout rate was high. You could quit at any time; some did and some were found unfit and were washed out. Only the best made it through. After thirty-four jumps from the tower and five jumps from a C-46 airplane, he finished the course. The silver wings looked good on his uniform. This was the late fall of 1952. Still just seventeen years old, he was thinking, *what an experience, what a life I'm living*, and this was only the first six months of army life. Of course, his thinking was, *anything beats picking cotton.*

Now on to Fort Bragg, North Carolina, and more training with the famous 82nd Airborne Division. So far, all the training seemed to gel together. What he had learned in basic training and airborne training was now making sense. He was being trained by officers and NCOs that were battle-tested veterans of World War II. They knew what they were talking about and these men of that not-so-distant war had the battle scars and medals to prove it.

Now on to bigger and more powerful weapons. Here, again, there was no room for error. You had to be fast and strong, and each shot had to be right on target every time; this was the real thing. Arvin had the right attitude, the right stuff. The training was demanding and again he could not get enough of it.

The Korean War was still going on and all his training was in preparation for combat. At that young age, now eighteen, he was eager and ready to go but knew that war was hell.

The headlines of all the newspapers were about the battles our brave men were engaged in: the Battle of White Horse, Triangle Hill, and later the Battle of Pork Chop Hill. Korea was an unforgiving country, so very cold in the winter time and scorching hot in the summer time. Arvin received orders for the 187th Airborne Regimental Combat Group and was now on his way to war. He was somewhere in between very excited and scared to death.

He was as well-trained as anyone could be for this assignment, ready to do his part. He was now a corporal with two stripes on his sleeve, a non-commissioned officer. This was going to be the first of so many tests he would face during the next twenty years of his military service. The big navy troop ship left San Francisco, California, and sailed across the Pacific Ocean. Two weeks later, it docked in Japan and there, with the 187th Airborne Group, they trained for war. On July 27, 1953, while standing in company formation, they were informed that the war was over. The pucker factor went away…what a relief!

Arvin, like all servicemen and women, trained very hard to be ready if they were needed. They would go if called and would give their very best when their best was needed. Yet, generally speaking, they are not crazy about going to war; most would agree that there are other ways of settling differences. War is hell.

The war was over, the armistice agreement was signed, but for Arvin the training continued; in fact, it never stopped. Airborne all the way—there was nothing better. Later he was promoted to sergeant. Now he was not only being trained; he was responsible for training others, teaching and leading by example about what it took to be one of the best.

In mid-1955, Arvin returned on leave and came back to Ryan Crossroads with a diamond for his high school sweetheart. She said yes. Then he came back home again in January 1956 and married her. Ms. Virginia Latham became Mrs. Virginia Briscoe. Eleven months later, a beautiful baby girl was born; they named her Debbie. This made life so much more enjoyable. Having a family was what he wanted most and, after fifty-six years of marriage, it is obvious they are still very much in love.

Just down the road at Fort Bragg, North Carolina, a very unique and highly trained unit was now excepting volunteers. The army Special Forces requirements were high; the testing, both mental and physical, was beyond the ability of an average person to pass. When one hundred men tested, only three had what it took to be accepted into the Special Forces training program. Arvin tested and was one of the three. Now he was in for the ride of his life. He could not foresee the real test that would challenge him to the fullest extent of his being over the next fifteen years.

Let me tell you about these special men and the training they go through.

Green Berets are three-time volunteers. First, they have to join the army on a voluntary basis and not be drafted. Secondly, they have to volunteer for airborne training and willingly jump out of perfectly good airplanes as part of that training. Thirdly, they have to volunteer for Special Forces. They are trained in broad military training and can serve as raiders in a direct-action role, but their primary role is that of a counterinsurgent and unconventional warfare force.

Author Dick Couch (a 1967 graduate of the US Naval Academy and former SEAL), in his book *Chosen Soldier*, describes the army Special Forces soldier as the most valuable individual on the battlefield. He goes on to say that the unconventional-warfare and counterinsurgency operations are difficult and nuanced and the warriors who practice this vital and demanding work are among our most skilled special soldiers.

Sergeant Arvin M. Briscoe
This picture was taken by Navy SEAL Chip Maury in 1967 over the island of Ieshima off the coast of Okinawa at about twelve thousand feet.

Arvin, the barefoot boy from Ryan Crossroads on Rural Route One, Joppa, Alabama, was now accepted into the most advanced training program the United States Army had to offer. Once he was awarded the beret, there remained a lot more training in a job specialty and in other areas, such as jungle warfare and survival training. In the end, these few, these Green Berets, were the boys next door, or down the road, now grown into men of honor and dignity, highly trained and motivated to go wherever their country needed them.

Arvin trained non-stop for twenty-four months, had endured and successfully passed each rigid test, and was now ready for any assignment. The army had invested so much time and money in him; he was ready. He wore the Green Beret proudly.

His first overseas assignment was with the 10th Special Forces Group at Flint Kaserne, Bad Tolz, Bavaria. This was a beautiful country, a perfect setting for the missions they were to undertake. Here his group trained to help and support resistance movements. This was the real thing during those days of Soviet postwar ambitions. He was, at a minute's notice, prepared to be deployed to the Middle East or even Africa.

No matter what assignment Arvin was given, no matter what mission he was on, he always…always wanted to be the best. He became a very skilled parachutist. Later he participated in the international parachuting competition for military personnel, much like the Olympics of today. He won the gold medal for the most accurate jumps. He was the forerunner of the famous Army Golden Knights parachute team.

Arvin continued his army career with the United States Army Special Forces and for the next fifteen years most of it was spent overseas: three tours in Viet Nam, two in Okinawa, an assignment at the West Point Academy as an instructor, and later as the non-commissioned officer in charge of Reserve Officers Training Candidates (ROTC) at the University of North Alabama. Each of these assignments is a story on its own.

Master Sergeant Arvin M. Briscoe Jr.

As I asked him about some of the men he served with and how they affected his life and his service, his face lit up. He mentioned Fred Zabitosky, who was presented the Medal of Honor. "What a privilege it was," he said, "to be invited to the White House for that occasion." There were so many others that are too numerous to mention here. He remembered the names of those men that came to his rescue when he was surrounded by enemy forces when it looked like there was no hope. Tears came easy as he mentioned some of his best friends who gave the ultimate sacrifice. They were truly a band of brothers. But, of all the people he admired the most, number one was his wife, Virginia, who had to endure his long absences over so many years and who kept the home fires burning. She waited, like the many other wives, not knowing if he would return alive or in a flag-draped casket. He thinks she is the real hero. I agree.

Arvin has 997 parachute jumps on his military records. But, off the record, he has another thousand, with many of them being HALO (high altitude low opening). A total of 1,997 jumps... WOW.

He surprised everyone by parachuting out of a single-engine airplane at forty-five hundred feet over Hulaco, Alabama, during a little league game. He said that was a fun jump as he was showing off to all the folks there that he grew up with. He landed right on target as he touched down at home plate. Everyone was very surprised to find out it was "Junior Briscoe," the kid who used to live just down the road.

So many times the people we take for granted, or the people we think we know who live on the same block as we do, or just down the country dirt road, are the ones who have put their lives on the line for our country and our freedom. They are heroes who went above and beyond the call of duty and you will never hear any of them say much about it.

When I start counting the medals Arvin earned over the twenty-one years of service, which include the Silver Star, three bronze stars, the Air Medal, and three army commendations, in all there are twenty-four. He was also awarded the Combat Infantrymen's Badge and the Master Parachutes Badge.

On May 29, 1996, at the Special Warfare Center, Fort Bragg,
North Carolina, Major General Tagney pins the Silver Star on
Master Sergeant Arvin M. Briscoe, Jr., twenty-five years
after the action.

Silver Star

ARVIN M. BRISCOE JR.

SERGEANT FIRST CLASS, UNITED STATES ARMY

For gallantry in action on 10 June 1968. SFC Briscoe was in command of a small US/Indigenous patrol conducting a combat mission deep within enemy held territory. SFC Briscoe and his men were on this mission, which entailed the recon of a known North Vietnamese Army Headquarters. Being aware that trail watchers were close behind him, SFC Briscoe continued his mission by closing within feet of the enemy soldiers. After the recon mission was completed, SFC Briscoe was en route to be extracted when there was contact with an enemy platoon of approximately 40 NVA soldiers. After being fired on, three of his men were wounded, two seriously. SFC Briscoe immediately moved to the front of his element to rescue his wounded men and issued orders to gain fire superiority and break contact. SFC Briscoe moved quickly through heavy enemy automatic weapons fire to rescue his wounded men and began carrying them one at a time away from enemy fire. SFC Briscoe continued to move his men through the dense jungle, carrying his wounded with him. SFC Briscoe, now with the enemy following closely behind him, used his radio to call for Tactical Air Support to equalize the pursuing enemy element. Now the enemy was moving to the right front of his element. The approaching enemy force was now on both his left and right. He knew that if he broke through the encirclement he would not be successful unless the wounded men were left behind; SFC Briscoe made the decision that none of his men would be left behind and now directed his men to set up a defensive perimeter. Immediately the enemy began assaulting his 12-man element from all sides. The deadly B-40 rockets landed and exploded in the midst of the small group, wounding seven more of his men. The enemy began closing on the small group with heavy automatic weapons fire that kept SFC Briscoe and his men pinned down. With just seconds to spare, the first TAC Air arrived on station. SFC Briscoe immediately marked his position and began calling for rockets on the heaviest side of the assault. The rockets for TAC were right on target, destroying and seriously wounding all the NVA on that side. SFC Briscoe began moving his men off the hill and then called for rockets on his old position, eliminating the entire enemy force. SFC Briscoe continued to move his men to safety; ten were wounded and three seriously. After being notified that rescue helicopters were en route, SFC Briscoe moved to an area where the canopy was fairly open and directed the helicopter to his position. While the helicopters were hovering above, SFC Briscoe attached his entire element to a McGuire rig; one by one, each soldier was lifted to safety. Now with his team safe, he was the last one to be extracted. SFC Briscoe's action and leadership saved his team; all twelve of his men came back alive. His actions bring great credit upon himself and the United States Army.

Signed,

Earl M. Simms

BG, USA THE ADJUTANT GENERAL

A note here: some of the soldiers he served with that I talked to think Master Sergeant Arvin M. Briscoe's actions while under enemy fire are most worthy of the Medal of Honor. I agree.

"You've never lived till you've almost died.

For those who fight for it,

Life has a flavor the protected will never know."

Special Operations Group motto

In August of 1973, Master Sergeant Arvin M. Briscoe retired after twenty-one years of continuous service to his country. He and Virginia live at 3711 Brazos Ct. SW, Decatur, Alabama, 35603-4625. I think they would appreciate hearing from all who read this. His home phone is 256-353-2504.

Arvin Briscoe Jr. was my neighbor on Rural Route One, Joppa, Alabama. He is the bravest man I have ever known.

When I grow up, I want to be just like him.

—William McDaniel McCollum

Arvin and Virginia

10

G ENERAL B OLDING

The sound of a horse at a slow gallop got my attention as I was walking home from the Hulaco store on this cool Saturday afternoon. I looked back and stopped to watch as the horse and rider came around the bend on that country dirt road. The rider slowed the horse to a trot and then stopped as he came up close to me.

He looked like a Confederate general sitting on his horse. The saddle was of the best leather, shiny and of the finest quality…it looked expensive. The horse was highly groomed, well-fed, and looked as if it could have been a race horse. I was so impressed. I was standing there in amazement admiring both horse and rider.

I had seen this man a couple of times at a distance but this was our first face-to-face meeting. I was in awe of him and his horse; I did not know what to say. His fine-blooded horse danced in, intelligent and quick, the nostrils aquiver, as if she was part-Arabian and quarter horse blood; she seemed actively proud of her rider. The horse was prancing around as if it was ready to get on down the road, anxious to run, yet the man calmed the horse and dismounted. He held out his big, calloused hand and said, "Hi, I am General Bolding." He stood at least six feet tall and weighed about two hundred pounds and it looked like he was all muscle. He had a strong, prominent chin, a touch of gray hair, a friendly look, and a soft voice. I felt like I had just shaken hands with the king of England or the president of the United States of America.

He said, "Son, let me see your hand again." He looked my hand over and said, "Where did you get those warts?" I said, "Sir, I don't know. They just appeared a few months back." He said, "Do you like warts?" I said, "No, sir." He then said, "Would you like for them to go away?" I said, "Yes, sir, I would." I was thinking, *what in the world is he talking about?* He mumbled something that I did not understand and said, "They will be gone in seven days." We talked for a few minutes then he got back up in the saddle, gave me one more look, and touched the brim of his hat with his right hand. The horse was raring to go. They rode away, the general sitting high in the saddle. The horse was kicking up dust and gravel as they rode out of sight.

I had forgotten to introduce myself. So much had happened: a general, his appearance, the horse, and the wart thing. I was so impressed with this event that I just plain forgot to mention my name.

I know I am easily impressed but in my mind this was special as this man stopped along the way and took the time to talk to me; that meant a lot to me. I wanted to get to know him better. He and his wife, Belle, lived up the road from our house in the hollow on Rural Route One. He farmed with two beautiful horses. They lived in a simple but very neat house. All the buildings were well taken care of. He was a really good farmer.

My grandpa McCollum used to tell me that people who take care of their livestock are usually good folks. General Bolding took lots of pride in his horses and very good care of all his animals. He was so much more than just a farmer. He knew just where to drill for water and could dig a well by hand with a pick and a shovel usually in less than two weeks. He loved being outside, loved to hunt, loved to sit around the camp fire and listen to the dogs run the fox…and he was a wonderful storyteller.

One time as I was walking past his house and he was outside splitting wood, he waved and motioned for me to come out to the wood pile. We talked for a few minutes then he asked if I would help him cut some fire wood. I said yes but first had to talk to my parents. He said okay and then wanted to know how much I would charge him. I said, "Mr. Dewitt pays me three dollars a day." He said that was fair and he would make sure I was well fed at the dinner table (noon meal). I thought, *whoa, that is a good deal*. I always enjoyed helping him as we cut wood and did other things around his farm. He was always showing me how to do things as if he was anxious to pass on all his knowledge to me. Even at that young age, I was thinking what a wonderful man and how lucky I was that he liked me.

He wanted me to help him rebuild a fence. I told him what day I could be there. I showed up early in the morning and we went to work. I was really going at it; he stopped me and said for me to slow down. He said, "I don't want you to wear out and for sure I don't want you to wear me out." Then he started telling me about fences. "Good fences make good neighbors," he said, "and the fence needs to be horse-high, pig-tight, and bull-strong." I thought to myself that *would be a good fence*.

After getting to know him better, I was thinking that he knew everything; there was not one question that he did not know the answer to. He knew how to predict the weather, even knew when a storm was coming and if it was going to be a bad one. He could tell at a distance what kind of tree each one was. He taught me how to make a wooden whistle, how to notch a tree so that it would fall just in the right place. He showed me how to saddle a horse; of course there was a right way and a wrong way. I do not know how much education he had but he was well blessed with tons of common sense. But the most important thing I learned from him was how to treat and get along with people. He said, "Always be careful what you say; you cannot unsay a cruel word." I never heard him utter a harsh word, never heard him use a dirty word, and he was the kindest man and so gentle. He was married to a wonderful lady. Mrs. Belle was a true Southern belle and the best cook ever.

Oh, yes…the warts started disappearing from my hand in less than seven days. I do not know what kind of power he had; do not know how he came about having that. I was in amazement then and still am today. But I did not question any of that. I was just glad that the ugly warts were gone.

AND here I must tell you that he was not a military general; that was not a title or rank. It was his name: General Lee Bolding. Over the years, I have never met anyone whose first name was General. As a young kid, I always thought of him as a man who wore stars on his shoulder…a real army general.

In the fall of 1961, I came back from Germany and was home on leave for a few days. I stopped by the Hulaco store and was wearing my army uniform. This was always a fun thing to do, just to see everyone, but more so just to show off my new sergeant strips. Mr. General Bolding was there and of course we had fun talking. He was telling me how proud he was of me and how good I looked in my uniform. I shook his hand and told him how much I appreciated him and all the great advice he gave me over the years. He said, "Yes, and I deserve a pat on the back for all that." He turned around and backed up close to me and I gave him a good pat on his back. The smile on his face was worth a million dollars. I have such wonderful memories of him.

As you can tell, he was one of my idols.

General Lee Bolding

Born July 1, 1892

Died Oct. 24, 1972

11

IT WAS A HENRY J

Living way out in the hills of North Alabama back in the '40s and '50s, not much traffic passed on those one-lane country, dusty, dirt roads. Not even one car would go past our house for days at a time. Back then, if we heard a car coming, we would stop what we were doing and look. We always waved even if we didn't know who it was. Farmers still do that today. If you don't wave then you are perceived as being not very friendly.

Most of the time we knew who owned the passing vehicle. We knew the color and make of each car. Everybody knew their neighbors' vehicles, and if a strange car or truck drove by, then we really gave it the once-over. We knew most all types of vehicles and who owned them. A Ford was so much different from a Chevrolet or a Plymouth. If one of our neighbors bought a new or different vehicle, he would drive by and show it off. Sometimes they would stop and let you get a good look at it. It was exciting, to say the least.

My friend John Ellenburg, Jr. introduced me to driving out in the hay field on a John Deere tractor. His sister, Martha Gale, taught me how to drive their pick-up truck when I was thirteen. I was hooked. I was always bugging them to let me drive, and they did but always in a safe place. I fell in love with driving.

I remember when our basketball coach, who was then about twenty-six years old, bought a new 1955 Chevrolet. What a beauty! It was a Saturday afternoon in late July. My brother and I were just leaving the Hulaco General Store. Coach Ralph had glass pack mufflers installed, and what a sound they made as he made a couple of passes by the store. Those glass packs were rumbling. We all were in awe as he showed off his pride and joy. I was thinking that some-day I would have a car just like his.

Most of us kids back then took pride in knowing all the makes, models, and years of cars, and we could easily tell them apart at a good distance. Then, all at once another car was going by from time to time, a car we just didn't know anything about or to whom it belonged. It was the first and only one I had at that time ever seen. It was so unique: small, and completely different in features from the Fords or the Chevys.

Later, I noticed that this small car was driving by and stopping at our mailbox. It was our mailman, Mr. Lige, who had this car that looked so different. Wow! Our very own mailman. Now we could put the puzzle together. Our mailbox was about a hundred yards from our house, out where two country roads met and one made a turn. This car was classy, neat, small, and even a different kind of color. It was just different. What kind of car was he driving? Of course, I just had to know.

The mailman came pretty much on time every day, so I had to figure out how I was going to be at the right place at the right time. The right place was our mailbox, but to be there at the right time was a little difficult. By the time I would see him, he had already delivered our mail. He was gone before I could get out to the old mailbox. I would be too far away. As you can see, this was eating at me. I was a nosey kid.

This was a new kind of car—not only new to me but to all of my friends. My friend Hilton said that he thought it was a cut-down ver-sion of the Studebaker. Billy Wayne, one of our neighbors who lived up the road from us, said he thought it looked like a Nash from a distance.

Our family had no type of motor vehicle, so for me to know about this car would be something up on my friends that I ran around with. I have always wanted to know everything. As a teenager, I wanted to know something that others did not. I was now on a mission.

One day, I had some free time about the time the mailman was to appear. The weeds were growing high around our mailbox. I took the old sling blade and started whacking the weeds down around it when the mailman approached. He pulled up, made a quick stop, waved, and just as I was about to start talking to him, he drove off, leaving me in a cloud of dust. He spent a total of two seconds at our mailbox. I just stood there with my mouth open, inhaling road dust.

For most of my life I have asked way too many questions, or at least that's what my parents told me a number of times. My thinking was, If you didn't know then ask someone. Now maybe that's okay, but it's not the question, mind you. It's how you ask the question that counts. It really is. Now, back to the wood pile and splitting wood. I had to come up with a plan, a plan to delay the mailman so that I could ask just the right questions.

Back then a postcard cost a penny; a first-class stamp was four cents. I thought if I stood there by the mailbox when he stopped, I could let Mr. Lige know that we needed a postcard and a stamp. That would delay him for a minute or two, and then I would have time to find out what kind of car he was driving. See how important this was to me?

The next day I went out and just waited for the mailman. Soon he came down the hill, dust flying everywhere. He made a quick stop, and I could tell he didn't have time to chit-chat.

I said, "Mr. Lige, I want to buy one stamp and a postcard." I gave him a nickel. I had my questions rehearsed in my mind. I said, "This is really a nice car. I am guessing that it cost a lot of money."

"Nope, it's a cheap car."

I said, "It looks really fancy."

"No, it's just a very simple, cheap car."

"Where did you buy it?"

"Sears and Roebuck."

His answer left me with my mouth open again. Sears and Roebuck was a mail-order catalog. Sears and Roebuck?

I asked again, "Sears and Roebuck?"

"Yes," he replied as he handed me the postcard and one stamp.

I had to act quickly. "What kind of a car is this?"

"A Henry J."

A Henry J? I had never in my life heard of such a car.

"Did you order it from Sears and Roebuck?"

He answered, "Yes."

I knew you could order all kinds of stuff from a mail-order cata-log, and it could be delivered right to your mailbox…but a car?

He said, "Little Will, see you later."

He sped away, and the road dust was everywhere.

I stood there thinking, just thinking. A Henry J. He ordered it from Sears and Roebuck. Did I hear that right? Now I had a hundred more questions.

Later, when I talked to Billy Wayne, I told him that the car the mailman drove was a Henry J.

He looked at me and said, "A Henry J?"

"Yes."

He said, "Will, are you sure?" He had never heard of a Henry J.

"Yep," I said. "It's a Henry J."

Later, I told Hilton the same thing and again he did not believe me as he said he knew all the cars, and for sure there was no such thing as a Henry J. I was now thinking that I was the only kid in the neighborhood that knew what a Henry J was.

Over the years, I have seen only a few Henry J's. It was a very simple car and you could only buy it new from Sears and Roebuck. So many more questions to ask about this car, but I felt that I was the first kid in that small community to know what a Henry J looked like.

About a year later, I was walking to the Ryan Country Store. Mr. Lige drove by and then stopped. He waited for me to catch up and then asked if I wanted a ride.

"Oh, yes," I said and climbed in. I was thinking about so many things as I sat in the passenger's seat, but the main thing I was think-ing was that I would love to drive this car. I had to word my next question just right. I said, "Mr. Lige, this is such a nice car, and some-day I would love to have a chance to drive a car like this."

He just looked at me as we both got out at the general store. He filled his car up with gas, and I went into the store. About ten minutes later I came back out with a twenty-five-pound sack of flour over my shoulder. I noted that he was still there…as if he was wait-ing for me.

He said, "Will, you want a ride back home?"

"My goodness, yes," I said.

He walked around and sat himself in the passenger's seat. I just stood there, wondering what was going on. He gave me a no-nonsense kind of look and said, "You're driving."

You know, it's the little things in life that you remember so much. My emotions were going every which way.

Mr. Lige knew I could drive, but he didn't know that I hadn't acquired a driver's license. I was only fourteen years old. I did not have the nerve to tell him. I was just thinking that this might be my only chance to drive this little car.

I will never forget that Saturday afternoon as I sat behind the wheel, cranked it up, and headed down the country road back to his house. I do not think we even talked. I just took my time and enjoyed the moment. Mr. Lige just watched as I must have looked like the happiest young man ever. I was in my glory, thinking what a lucky kid I was. The memory of that day will never leave me. He trusted me with his one and only car. It was a Henry J.

12

FOX HUNTERS
AND CAMP FIRES

I was on a fast walk down the hill; it was late, about 10:00 p.m. on a Friday night. This dirt road I had traveled a hundred times, it seemed, at this late hour of the night was always a bit scary. This was the first night of our basketball season at Ryan High School. After the game, I had to stay and clean up the gym, the hallway, and both the men's and women's bathrooms, empty all the trash, and make sure the high school building was locked up. This was in the middle of September 1956; I was fifteen years old. I did not like walking home this late at night.

I could feel my heart beating, could hear my foot steps on the one-lane dirt road. It was always like this for me. It was coal black, I could only see a slight view of the road, yet I knew at all times where I was. I knew where each bend in the road was and even knew where the spot was where they found a dead man in the ditch along the side of that one-lane road a few years back. Can you see why I was scared? About halfway down the hill, I heard a noise. It sounded like a small animal running through the woods and across the road ahead of me…I wondered what that could be as my heart beat even faster. Off in the distance, I could hear dogs barking and in just a few minutes they were crossing the road behind me, chasing the animal. Now I knew it had to be fox hounds running the fox. I was somewhat relieved.

Just down the dirt road I could see a light. As I kept walking, I could hear voices and again I was a bit apprehensive and knew that nothing good happens to people out that late at night. Around one more bend, then the fork in the road, across the bridge, and I would be home.

As I got closer, I could see a campfire in the fork of the road and a few guys sitting by the fire. *Should I keep walking or should I stop and say hi?* As I got closer, I could hear the voice of Mr. Ed Jarrett, one of our neighbors. What a relief it was to know who was there at that campfire. He was a fox hunter. I did not know what would happen if I just walked up among them; would I scare them? So I decided to start singing so they would know it was a human being walking down the road and I hoped they would not shoot me. My voice did not cooperate. It sounded like someone was choking me; it was the worst rendition of "Jesus Loves Me" that had even been sung. They all turned and looked at me…I knew they were thinking, *what in the world is wrong with that kid?*

I walked up and sat down on a log by Mr. Jarrett and now I felt safe. I looked around and there was Mr. Boyd Alvin Flack, Mr. General Bolding, Mr. Prince St. John, and Preacher Henry Mooney. They wanted to know what I was doing out this late at night. I told them I was coming home from a basketball game. Mr. Ed wanted to know if we won or lost; I said we won by two points. Of course, I had to explain how it all ended. I tried to tell all this with excitement in my voice.

I told them that we were tied with about ten seconds left to play. Hubert Allen brought the ball up the court and he was heavily guarded by two players he came across the center line as the clock was ticking down. J.C. made a move to the sideline and faked out the guy guarding him then he made a move to the inside. Hubert made a bounce pass to him and, with two seconds left, J.C.'s jump shot bounced off the back board and went through the hoop as the buzzer sounded.

I told them everyone went crazy. Preacher Mooney said that it sounded like the ball game was much more exciting than fox hunting.

I sat there for a while just listening to them talk; I must say I was enjoying myself. Sitting around a campfire was a wonderful thing back then…still is today. But being there with these fox hunters was something else. Off in the distance the dogs were running; each had a different bark and each hunter could tell by the sound if it was his dog. Most of the fox hound breeds were called "walkers"; back then, a good fox hound would bring a pretty good price, somewhere around twenty-five dollars or more.

Then all at once the dogs were heading back to where we were sitting. The dogs were really running and barking as if they were right on the tail of the fox. They were getting closer and closer, the guys were quiet, and Mr. Boyd Alvin said, "It sounds like Ole Blue is leading the pack." Preacher Mooney said, "Sounds more like the fox is making a loop crossing back over his old trail." General Bolding agreed and said, "If that happens then the hunt is over for the night." A fox is one smart animal. It knew that if it circled back and across its own trail, the dogs would be confused over which trail to follow, then the fox would be way ahead of the pack. Have you ever heard the phase "dumb like a fox"?

About fifteen minutes later, it was all quiet. The guys were not saying much; they knew it was over. Then the dogs started coming in. Each one was pretty much tired out. They curled up close to their owners and lay down. It was getting really late; I said goodnight and headed to the house. What a night.

I knew about fox hunting, knew about the hounds and the men who loved this kind of sport…if that is what it is called. This was a first for me. I liked all of this for the main reason that there was no killing involved. In almost every case, the fox outran the hounds. There are so many different kinds of music but the sound of a good dog chasing a fox is something to behold. All the fox hunters I knew were good men, the kind of folks that you would like to have as neighbors. I wanted so much to do that again. I wanted to sit on a log by the campfire and listen to the dogs run. Maybe they had a little nip of moonshine, maybe they smoked, chewed, and spit tobacco juice in the fire, but that made it even more exciting for me as I watched the campfire burn and listened to those men talk about the fox and their hounds.

And now one last thought as I walked on down the dirt road through the darkness to our house. I was smiling as I had on this cool night set around a campfire with a general, a prince, and a preacher. That was my thinking: what a lucky kid I was.

Campfires and fox hunters, their dogs and the fox...these memories of those yesterday years will never fade from my mind.

13

GEORGIA CREDIT CARD

The car was traveling pretty fast as it passed me then slowed down and spun around and came back again. I was wondering what in the world was going on. As the car came back up behind me then stopped, the passenger rolled down the window and said, "Hey, you wanna ride?" It was around 9:00 p.m. I thought that was nice that they asked me. I was on my way home after a basketball game and it was starting to get cold. It had not been a good evening for me. I had set on the bench for the entire game for four long quarters and did not get to play. The coach was a bit upset with me as I had missed two practices, yet I was hoping that he would let me play for a few minutes. I needed to be walking off my anxiety, my uneasy feelings. But I just could not turn down a ride home at this late hour.

At first I was not sure who all was in the car. I got in, closed the door, and, to my surprise, a guy by the name of Henry was driving. Of all the students in our small school, he was the one that had bullied me from time to time. He weighed about two hundred pounds and I weighed about one-forty and he was two years older than I was. I was thinking that maybe I should get back out and keep on walking but we were now headed down the road. I had no idea what might happen and was hoping that they would not take me out on a back road and beat the crap out of me.

The other guy was Cecil; both knew where I lived and they both knew what road to take to get me home. At first I was not paying much attention to where they were going. Then I noticed that they drove up to the road that I lived on then turned the opposite way. I said, "Where are you taking me?" They said, "We need gas." By then I was thinking I needed to get out of that car…the sooner, the better. At this time of the night and out in the country, there were no gas stations that were open…not even one.

I was thinking now I was in trouble and was getting scared. Over the past year or so I wanted so much to get even with Henry but knew this was not the time or place for that. I was in the back seat and could easily have punched him in the head or could have gotten a good chokehold on him. Everything was going through my mind. I don't think I would have ever tackled him…but I was thinking it.

Cecil looked back at me and asked if I knew how to use a Georgia credit card. A what? I had never heard of such a thing. My answer was, "No. What is a Georgia credit card?" He then said, "We will get you home but first we need for you to help us get some gas." I was thinking, *me!?*

Henry was now driving down one road then back up another. The other guy, Cecil, said he would show me how to use the Georgia credit card. I knew by now they were up to no good and I had to put my thinking cap on and figure a way out of this sad situation. Cecil showed me an old rubber garden hose, which was about five feet long, and a five-gallon gas can and said, "This is how to do it." I said, "Okay, I got it." I was lying.

They were talking about which farm would be the best, the easiest and least likely place not to get caught. They mentioned a couple but now I had an idea. We had driven by Mr. Dewitt Crawford's place and I could see that the lights were still on in his house. I said, "Drive by the Crawford place and let me out. I know where his M Farmall farm tractor is parked." They stopped the car and I got out with the hose and five-gallon gas can. I said, "Give me about fifteen or twenty minutes and pick me up here at the same spot." They left and drove away. I ran as fast as I could to Mr. Dewitt's house, knocked on the front door, and then told him what was going on. Mr. Dewitt was our landlord. He smiled and said, "By gad, we will take care of them." He told me to go fill the gas can with water and go back out on the road. He gave me instructions on what to do and said, "Make sure you do just what I have told you…and follow my instruction to a T." I said, "Okay." We had a plan.

I headed back down the road carrying that heavy gas can full of water. Here they came without their lights on. The car stopped and Henry said, "Way to go, McCollum." I said, "We need to get this in the gas tank so there will be no evidence." They said that was a great idea. I took the gas cap off and emptied the whole five-gallon can into the tank. A truck came down the road while I was doing all this. Hey, I was caught red-handed. It was Mr. Dewitt. The plan was working great.

He came up and took the gas can and the rubber hose and told me to get in his truck. He made sure they knew how disgusted he was with them and me…more so me, because I was the one who supposedly stole the gas. He went up to their car; of course he knew who they were and told both of them he would be talking to their parents about all this. I do not know what all he told them, but for sure he was doing all the talking.

He came back to his truck, looked at me with a grin, got his pipe out, and lit it; we just sat there and watched as Henry and Cecil drove away. He said, "They won't be going far." He gave me a pat on the shoulder and said, "Good thinking, Will, and a good job." Mr. Dewitt was talking more than he usually does…he was thinking that our plan worked perfectly. We had a good talk as he drove me home. Everything turned out well: Mr. Dewitt now had an almost new, free, five-gallon gas can and I enjoyed the ride home. Sometimes the harder the lessons learned in life, the easier it is to remember them.

Mr. Dewitt later told me the car stopped about two hundred feet down the road and three days later it was towed to a local garage and there it set for about two weeks with the gas tank off and the hood up. We both laughed about this for the longest time. I still sometimes laugh out loud when I remember about that night and the Georgia credit card.

Five gallons of gas back then would have cost about a dollar. I wondered how much it cost to tow the vehicle and to take the gas tank off, clean it out, and put it back together? I later heard through the grapevine that they could never get the engine to run right again. Most of the time what goes around comes around.

From that time on I forgot about getting even with Henry. Every once in a while he would give me the evil eye and then the biggest grin ever would come across my face. I just couldn't help myself.

Sweet revenge.

14

CROOKED CREEKS
AND MOONSHINERS

The man stepped out from behind the tree with a double-barreled shotgun and confronted me. He scared the living jeebees out of me then he asked, "What are you doing out here in this part of the woods?" He did not give me time to answer; he then said for me to go back the way I came and not to be out there snooping around. I said, "Sir, I was not snooping but just out looking for some wild poke salad." He said, "Turn around and start walking." I was scared to death thinking he might shoot me in the back. But for sure I never forgot that and I NEVER went back to that area again. This was in the early 1950's. Some lessons in life you learn very quickly.

It was a known fact back then that there were people living around us who were moonshiners. I do not know for sure if I could have named them, but most of us had a pretty good idea who they were. But that was okay...or at least that was the way most of us felt back then. They did not bother us and we did not bother with them. We hoed and picked cotton and made a poor living doing that; they made homemade whisky and it appeared that they were doing better than we were. Of course, you don't have to worry none about the lawmen coming around and hauling you off to jail when you are picking cotton.

Our house there in the hollow sat between two creeks. One of them ran through our pasture out behind the old barn. The creek curved around through our pasture and then down into gullies, curving away from our farm, making its way to a larger creek. It was a shallow, slow-moving, crooked creek about two or three feet deep and about ten feet wide. The creek zigzagged through very dense forest. The trees overlapped the slow-moving water as it moved on down the valley. Our livestock drank from this creek, wading out into the running water, drinking and doing all the things cows and pigs do while standing in the creeks. During the hottest days of summer, the hogs and cattle would from time to time wade out and just lie down in the water to cool off. Us kids would find a place upstream where the water was clear and take a bath.

The other creek, which was about the same size, ran along one of our fields and made its way downhill and about a half-mile through the wooded valley, where they both joined together. This was back-woods, wild country, mostly out in the middle of nowhere. This was moonshine country: a good place to hide all the materials that were needed to make homemade whisky.

The crooked creeks were good places to wade, a good place to catch minnows, and a good place to go fishing. Mostly, just a cool place to sit in the shade and watch the water rumble over the stones and dream about catching a big one. For all of us kids, we were living a dream, so peaceful and quiet and we had no idea what was going on up- or downstream…and for the most part, at that young age, we didn't care.

I remember one time a car drove up into our yard; a couple of guys got out and came out to the barn, where we were working. They asked permission to walk through the woods where our farm was. My dad very quickly told them that they would have to go talk to Mr. Dewitt Crawford as he was the land owner. I could tell that my dad did not want to be seen talking to them. He later said he thought they were revenuers. I think for the most part they went pretty much where they pleased without permission from anyone; of course they were lawmen. You had to be careful who you talked to…or were seen talking to.

I just could not figure out how they could hide all that and conceal the site where all the manufacturing of that illegal homebrew was being made. First of all, they needed to get all the supplies to the location then get the boiler there. That had to be a job just doing all that. Back then they used wood to heat the boiler and I always wondered where that smoke went. I am sure that all that had to be a little bit smelly. They used the same water that came from the creek where the cattle and hogs stood and wallowed and did what animals usually do when standing in the water. Plus the same water we used to bathe and swim in. To me, that did not sound like a very healthy thing. I might have seen all this differently if I were involved with this task or depending on the sales for a living. These moonshiners knew what they were doing and I think they were pretty good at it.

One time I was with a few guys about my own age and they were passing the jug around; for the life of me, I could not partake of that. It was not that I was so goodie-goodie. I was thinking about those hogs wallowing in the creek water that was used to make that moonshine. I remember the cows standing out in the creek and later seeing cow pies floating downstream and us swimming and, of course, peeing in the water.

I ventured down this road one time just to see if this sort of thing might be for me, but on a much smaller scale. It was late spring; the blackberries were plentiful. My friend Hilton and I decided to make some homemade blackberry wine. I picked the blackberries; Hilton obtained the sugar and yeast and the rest of the stuff we needed to make the wine. We mixed all that up, poured everything into a mason jar, wrapped a clean rag over the top of the jar, and hid it out in the woods along the creek bank. He said it had to ferment. I said, "Ferment?" In other words, it had to rot. He said, "Yep." I thought, *Okay*. A few days later, he and I went to check on it; the blackberry juice was in the fermenting stage and was oozing out the top and I could not believe all the bugs, spiders, flies, bees, and a hundred other insects that were crawling all over the jar. I told Hilton, "We can't drink that stuff." He said, "Ah, don't worry...that's what makes it good." I have never cared much for wine.

We lived in a dry county, meaning that no type of alcoholic beverages could be sold. I think for the most part that was a good thing for the moonshiners. I am guessing that they had lots of customers. Like all businesses, each was trying to outdo the other. The local folks knew who made the best shine. I think back then it was a trade that spread by word of mouth…imagine that.

As a young kid, I thought about which was better: working on the poor farm, hoeing and picking cotton, or getting into the bootlegging business. After pondering that for a while, it was a no-brainer. You didn't have to worry about getting arrested for picking cotton.

15

A JOCK STRAP...A WHAT?

Growing into the teenage years is both exciting and challenging for kids. For me, it was exciting just to say that I was a teenager. Like saying, "Hey, now I am grown up and now I know almost everything that I need to know and, for the most part, I know more than everybody else." Anyway, that was who I was being: the big brother of our clan. I would not, nor could not, pass up the opportunity to brag about all the knowledge I had to my younger brothers and sisters, even though they did not give a hoot about what all I knew...or what I thought I knew.

Well, I think my thinking was pretty much like that back in 1954–'55. I was thirteen going on fourteen years old. I was well into being a teenager; fourteen years old is getting up there, you know. I was now on the Ryan School's junior basketball team. I had a number; the big "12" was on the front and back of my red and black Ryan basketball jersey. The trunks were red with a black stripe down the legs. I was the proudest kid you had ever seen. Now I had a uniform...I have always liked uniforms.

Coach Ralph told me to keep it clean, keep it looking good. He said always iron the shirt after washing it. He wanted me to look sharp in the Ryan basketball uniform. And one more thing he said: "Be sure when you wear this uniform, always wear a jock strap." A... jock strap. A jock strap? I knew a little bit about history, had all the United States presidents' names memorized, but what in the heck was a...jock strap?

For sure, I did not want to ask any of my friends what it was. So I started asking them some small-type questions like, "Do you have a…jock strap?" J.C., my friend, gave me that look and said, "Of course." I asked Hubert T. what kind he had. He said, "There is only one kind." I wanted to ask John, another one of my friends, to let me see what his looked like, but I just did not have the nerve. Later, as we practiced in our school gym, most of us wore just what we went to school in…or at least that is what I wore. Back then, we did not have gym shorts or shirts. So I asked Coach Ralph where I could buy one of those things. He said the next time I was in Arab to stop at the clothing store on Main Street; they had them.

Of course, I had no money and, for the most part, my family had no money, so I had to ask my mom to ask my dad for enough money to buy a jock strap. She said, "A jock strap?" She looked at me as if I had asked her for the money to buy an exotic animal. She stopped what she was doing and started asking me all kinds of questions.

"What is a jock strap?"

"Heck, I don't know."

"Why do you need a jock strap?"

"I don't know."

"What is it for?"

"I don't know."

All I could tell her was that Coach Ralph said I needed one. She said, "Did Coach Ralph give you the money to buy a jock strap?" Of course she knew the answer to that question before she asked me.

She wanted to know how much one of them straps cost. I really did not know but I thought that it was about five dollars… She said, "Five dollars?" like I had just asked her for all of her egg money…and rightly so, for that was pretty much everything she had saved from selling eggs to the peddler for the past few weeks. Five dollars was a lot of money then…and more so for us.

While growing up, I was told over and over again that I could not have things that my other siblings could not have. So I had to sell my mom on the idea of something I really needed even though I had no idea what it was or what it was for. And why in the world did I need one of those things anyway? Where was Coach Ralph when

I really needed him? I was beside myself trying to explain all this to my mom. With this subject, I knew nothing...down deep inside I knew I was dumber than a fence post. She said she would talk to my dad and see if we could afford that. I thought, *Here we go again*.

The next morning, after I did chores and now was ready to catch the big yellow school bus, Mom gave me two one-dollar bills, eight quarters, and a bunch of nickels, dimes, and pennies. It was a sad time as I knew that was all the money she had...and now I had taken it to buy something that I still did not know what it was for. She was not a happy lady for sure.

I told Mom that I would go to the store after school and get one and would be home just as soon as I could to do all my chores. All day long I was not with it at school. Just the idea of how all this might end up...I wished I could have just had my mom go to Arab and buy one for me. Not a chance.

After school I caught a ride to Arab and went to the clothing store on Main Street. There was only one person in the whole store and it was a lady...a lady. She met me right inside the front door as if she had been waiting all day for me to show up. She was smiling and then asked me if she could help me. I would have liked to have talked to a man but she was the only one there at this time. I have always liked the smell of that country clothing store, but now I was beginning to sweat. Talking to a strange lady about a jock strap was not an easy thing for me back then...maybe even so now.

I told her, as I looked down at my shoes, that I needed to buy a jock strap, and she said, "Athletic supporter?" I looked over at the men's shirts on the rack and said, "No, a jock strap." She gave me that look that said, "Little boy, you are messing with my mind" and told me to follow her. In the back of the store were all kinds of sporting items. She asked me what size I needed. *Here we go again*. Heck, I did not know. She looked at me and then said, "The sizes come in small, medium, and large." I looked around as I still did not want to look at her. I said, "Could I look at one?" She got one off the rack and showed it to me. Of course, this was the first time I had ever seen such a thing. It looked so skimpy. Was this what I needed? There was nothing to it...nothing. Just a piece of cloth with some straps. Was this it? I was, at that time, close to six feet tall and weighed about 140 pounds and I was sweating.

I was now plowing in new ground, as we said there on the farm. I had no idea what I was looking at, did not know what size, or even if I would be able to figure out how to put it on. I asked the lady if I could try it on. She very quickly said, "NO." Okay. I wanted to ask her what size would she suggest, but there are some questions that you just do not ask a lady. Doggone it; I had to make a decision. This thing was in a package and there was no way to size it up. I asked her how much it cost and she said, "Three dollars plus tax." That was good news as now my mom would be getting some of her egg money back.

I gave her the money and took a small one…I had no idea if it was the right size. How would I? The package did say "athletic support," and I was hoping that it was the same as a jock strap. I paid her then I was good to go and ready to get the heck out of there. As I was about to leave the store, I decided maybe I should get a medium. If it was too big, maybe I would grow…well, that was my thinking. At least I had a jock strap, a.k.a. athletic supporter. The lady was not happy with me as she had to go back and get a medium and take the small one back. I wondered what she was thinking…maybe I did not want to know what she was thinking. I just wanted to get out of there with that thing in a paper sack and get back home.

Now, back home…

Generally, when anyone in our family bought something new, every one of the family wanted to see it. If you got a new shirt, you had to put it on and show it off; even a pair of blue jeans, you had to put them on and come into the living room and show them off. When one of my sisters purchased a new dress or when Mom made them something new, they would go put it on and come out into the living room and show it off. Everyone would "ohhh" and "ahhh," and it was a big deal for sure. All my brothers and sisters knew that I had gone to town to buy something. They had no idea what it was… kinda like a secret, and that made them even nosier. In fact, it was kind of a secret even for me as I was still not so sure what it was…I only had a general idea.

Then I did the dumbest thing ever...I mean ever! I left it on the table in the living room in that paper sack, right in plain sight.

I had chores to do, wood to cut so Mom could start a fire in the wood-burning cook stove, hogs to slop, and also two cows to milk... by hand, of course. I laid the paper sack on the table in our living room, changed into my work clothes, and went out to do chores as I had to hurry because I was now late getting started. I should have hid it under the bed or have taken it to the barn or done something with it as everyone was so nosey. I couldn't believe they would be that interested...well, thinking back, I should have known.

By the time I got all my chores finished and went back into the house, this thing was no longer in the paper sack. My brother Conley and a couple of my nosey sisters were passing it around; even my mom was in on it. My sister Fran and I were always fighting; she thought I had an attitude problem, and I thought she had a mouth problem...she still has a mouth problem. She wanted me to open it up and let everyone see what was inside. No way. By now my brother Thomas Randolph had it and was waving it around over his head and singing or trying to sing the dumbest song ever.

Hey, brother Will, setting on a sill, let us all see, with this thing on, how you gonna pee.

He was singing that over and over again, and then all the rest joined in. Now I was mad at all of them and red in the face. I was ready to take all of them on in a fight.

Anyway, I snatched that thing away from them and took off to the bedroom to see how it worked. What an ugly thing it was; even though it was a medium, it was so darn small-looking. I got it out of the plastic bag and looked at it. There was nothing to it; just a few straps hooked on to a piece of cloth...that was it. And it cost three dollars. What a rip-off! By this time my brothers Conley and Thomas were standing in the bedroom looking at me, and they did not want to leave. What a nosey family I was born into! I ushered them out and tried to try it on. It took a while to figure it out, and after I did, I was not so sure I had it on right. First I got my legs through the wrong straps, and then I tried it on another way, and it just did not feel right at all. By now I was wondering if I had paid good money for the wrong thing. Was this thing really a "jock strap"? Was this what Coach Ralph wanted me to wear? It sure did not look right nor did it feel right. This was not going like I thought it would…and for sure I had no idea how I thought it would go. A couple of more tries and I was pretty sure I had it figured out, but not really sure. The first time I wore it in a game I had one of the straps in the wrong place. You do not need to know how I knew.

Anyway, I put my britches back on and hid that thing under the mattress then I went out to the living room. My nosey brothers and sisters were just setting and standing, waiting for me. All of them had that look on their face as if they were expecting me to come out and model it with a big ole smile on my face…or at least that is what I thought they were thinking. Now it was about suppertime, and Fran had the bright idea that I should put it on and set at the supper table. They did not know what it was nor did they even have an idea, but they knew it was something that only guys wore. Why was there so much concern? Yet they knew it was kind of a secret or something. Conley, T.R., and even Lena Elizabeth thought that was a splendid idea. Fran and I got into it; everyone was giving me a hard time. Now it was suppertime, and all of us were at the table, everyone giving me the evil eye, smirking at me. My dear ole mom just sat there and did not come to my rescue; she had that crooked smile on her face. I don't know if she was having too much fun with all this or if she was just happy to have some of her egg money back…I think more so the egg money.

For weeks I did not hear the last of this ordeal; even today my sisters think it was so darn funny and I think they have told everyone in the whole world about the skimpy underwear that I had to wear just to play basketball. And Thomas Randolph was still asking me, "William, how in the world are you gonna pee with that thing on?"

16

Coon on a Log

The blue tick hound and a five-dollar shotgun

I asked the guy, "What is the cheapest gun you have?" He looked around for a while and said he had a single-barrel twelve-gauge for eight dollars. He found it and was showing it to me. He must have had at least fifty different types of guns. He let me look at it while he was talking to the people who were passing by. This was a very busy place. I only had five dollars.

In the 1950s, most of my friends had a gun to hunt with and to target practice with, but more so just to say they had a gun. I wanted one, too—not just a family gun but my very own gun. I was at an event at Scottsboro, Alabama. This small town was about thirty-five miles from where we lived. It was two or three events wrapped into one. It was a gun show, flea market, swap event, and the main show was called a "coon on a log."

Back in 1956, this was a first for me. I was now fourteen years old. I was excited just to be there with at least two hundred people and it looked like just as many dogs. I had never in my life seen so many dogs. All of them were coon dogs. I was there with my friend Larry and was surprised that he knew so much about this event and about coon dogs. He would point out the breeds to me. There were "black and tans," "treeing walkers," "redbones," "blue ticks," and so many that looked like mixed breeds. I was impressed, to say the least.

I think you could buy anything, from a pick-up truck to a two-hundred-dollar coon dog…the pick-up truck might have been cheaper. This was the best trade show ever, so exciting and so much going on, and the main event was yet to come.

Again, this was a first for me. I wanted to see everything and visit each table and go into every tent and see what all was for sale. I could hear guys talking about trading one item for another. One guy was trying to get a good deal on a .22-caliber rifle. I was all ears as it was interesting to see how the buyer and seller came to a price. I was getting a good lesson in marketing 101 and it was fun.

I was still thinking about that eight-dollar shotgun.

Later I saw this lady with a really nice blue tick coon dog. Larry said, "Boy was that ever something to look at." I said, "The dog?" He said, "No, dummy, the lady." She had light brown hair and was the only lady I had seen at this event with a coon dog and, boy, was she pretty. Of course, she was an older lady. She had to be at least thirty years old. The blue tick looked like a show dog. We would be seeing both of them later by the pond.

All at once I could hear dogs barking, like fifteen or twenty dogs all barking at the same time. These coon dogs really knew how to bark; it sounded like they had something treed. They were excited. Now most of the people were starting to move down to where all the commotion was. Larry said, "I think the big show is about to start."

We could now see the area where the event was going to take place. Just down the park from where we were at was a small pond with a floating platform, about ten feet square, out in the middle. On the platform were a couple of guys and some wire cages with raccoons inside. About eight feet from the floating platform was a log about four feet long and about two feet around. The log was just barely in the water.

By now, the dogs and their owners were at the edge of the pond. They all had registered their dogs and each dog had a number. The dogs knew what was going on and each one was getting excited; you could tell by the way they were carrying on. Never in my life have I ever owned a hound dog and I have never gone coon hunting. I knew about coon hunting, but this was all new to me. It was fun just watching them as their owners were trying to control their dogs. Each one had a different bark. It was a special kind of music that only hunters might appreciate.

The area around the pond was marked off. The spectators were in one area, the judges and the timekeepers in another. Standing in the back of a pick-up truck was a guy who was the announcer with a loud speaker. He was the one who controlled the event; he knew everything about all this. He was good at that. He would have a little story about each dog and the owner. He knew how to keep the show going and make it exciting.

I think the order that the dogs would go in the water was chosen at random. The crowd was excited, the dogs were excited, and I couldn't wait to see how this was going to unfold. The announcer talked about the rules, about safety, and then pointed to one of the judges and asked if they were ready. Then he pointed to the floating platform and said the same thing. I looked out and by now the coon was on the log. The coon had a harness on and the guys on the platform had a small chain connected to the harness. All the dogs and owners were lined up in order. The first dog up was howling to go. The timekeeper looked at the owner and said, "Is your dog ready?" He said, "Ready." The whistle blew and the dog lunged into the water, as it was barking that coon dog bark, and away he went to get that coon.

I do not remember all the rules about this event. The dog had to get the coon off the log within a set time...I think two minutes. It takes a good dog to do that. The raccoon can mess up a dog's face and, once in the water, can drown the dog in a minute. Here I must say I like dogs much more than I like raccoons. The raccoon can tear up a dog in a minute; the dog just has to be smarter.

The first dog, number 27, was a blue-ribbon winner of some past event. The dog was swimming out, barking and carrying on, and went straight for the coon on the log. I looked around at the folks standing 'round me and could not tell who was the most excited, the people or the dog...or maybe the raccoon.

Number 27 went for the coon, the coon backed away and swatted him in the face, and the dog yipped and backed away. Now he had second thoughts. He swam around looking for a better angle. The coon kept an eye on the dog as if to say, "You wanna try that again?" The dog was looking for a better angle; he swam around to the other side and went for the coon again and just about got his nose torn off. That was it. The coon was taken off the log and the owner called him back. Number 27 would not get a ribbon today... only a bloody nose.

The next dog up did not do any better; in fact, once he got slapped in the face with those sharp claws, he just swam around barking at the coon. The whistle blew and that was it for him. I think for the most part the two guys on the platform did everything they could do to make sure that the coon or the dog was not seriously injured, or it appeared that way to me.

Now about thirty minutes into this event, not one dog was successful in displacing that coon from the log. One dog got his face torn up pretty bad as he could not outsmart the raccoon. Next up was number 44 and it was the pretty lady with the blue tick. I moved on down, trying to get closer to the edge of the pond. I heard two guys talking about this lady and her dog. One of the guys said her husband had lost both of his legs and one arm in the Korean War. The other fellow said that he was awarded the Medal of Honor. At that time, I did not know anything about how special that medal was. But I knew just by the name "Medal of Honor" it had to be something really special. The blue tick dog had been given to him as a puppy when he came home.

I was now more interested in the pretty lady with the blue tick. Larry said that her dog was more of a pet than a hunting dog. He said, "You want to bet that five dollars?" I was thinking about it. Anyway, the timekeeper said, "Are you ready?" She said, "Yes." The whistle blew and the blue tick went nuts. Number 44 was a fast swimmer and went straight for the coon on the log. He swam out to the coon then around and back under the log and, in less than a minute, the coon and the dog were in the water. The crowd went wild as it really was a fun thing to see. The official time was forty-seven seconds. I looked at Larry and was now wishing I would have taken his bet.

The man on the platform separated the coon and the blue tick and it looked like neither was injured. The lady called her dog back. As number 44 swam back to her, all at once the dog ran to this fellow who I had not seen before. He was sitting in a wheelchair. The dog started running and jumped into his lap. He went one way and the wheelchair went the other way. They both were on the ground. He was hugging the dog and it looked like the dog was hugging him. The lady came over and all three sat on the ground hugging each other as the people all stood up and were cheering them. It was a sight to see.

That really made my day. The blue tick was awarded the blue ribbon and the lady was presented with a hundred-dollar check. Larry said we had better get going as we needed to catch a ride back home. I said, "Let's walk by and see if that eight-dollar shotgun is still there." He said, "Let me have your five dollars; let me see if I can get that gun for you." We stopped and, sure enough, it was still there. Larry told the guy that we were leaving and going back home. He said he would like to buy that shotgun but only had five dollars. The guy said, "Make it six and it is yours." Five dollars was a lot of money. Larry said, "Well, we better be going." We walked out and the fellow hollered and brought the gun out to us and Larry gave him five one-dollar bills. I could not believe it. Larry said, "You never know until you try." I learned another good lesson about marketing.

Now we were back out on the highway: two kids hitchhiking, one with a shotgun. We caught a ride back to Hulaco. We stopped at the store and showed off my gun and then we walked home. What a day.

I wonder what would happen today if two kids were walking or hitchhiking on a highway with a gun…I wonder.

This was the first and last time that I had ever been to an event like this. But I was happy that I now had a gun. My mom was not impressed. "Five dollars wasted," she said. I loved that gun; I cleaned it, admired it, and could not wait to shoot it. We had a few old shot-gun shells in the trunk. The first time I tried to shoot it, the shell did not explode then the next one…and bang! But the gun came unbreached and the empty shell hit me in the head and, boy, did that hurt. Each time I shot, it would come unbreached. I was now thinking about what my mom said about wasting money. I was afraid and thinking that I might really get hurt. So I oiled it, wrapped it, and put it away; over the years, I had completely forgotten about it. A few years back I found out that my little brother John had taken a liking to that gun. Now, sixty years later, he still has it. He had it repaired and refurbished and he says it is one of his prized guns.

The trade show, the coon on a log, the lady with the blue tick coon hound, and the five-dollar shotgun. So many memories from Rural Route One.

17

GHOST STORIES

"It was blood red," he said. I looked over at my brother Conley and his eyes was as big as a saucer and he did not blink as if he could not believe what he just heard. Blood red. I looked across the table. My little sister Fran, who was still eating, had now scooted as close to Mom as she could. On one hand, I wanted him to continue and, on the other, I was not so sure I wanted to hear the rest of the story.

My grandpa McCollum came to visit us often and sometimes stayed for a week or more at a time. He was well-liked by most everyone. All of us loved having him at our house. At six feet, six inches tall, he towered over everyone. He was a storyteller who loved to sit and talk about the good ole days. He loved to tell all kinds of stories that he said were true. None of us ever doubted that they weren't.

At the supper table, it was fun to hear our parents and our grandpa talking about so many different subjects: the past, politics, farming, and about the war still going on in Korea. We sometimes lingered for a goodly amount of time after eating supper, just setting there talking. My mom did not allow any smoking at the kitchen table. Grandpa and my dad smoked but to do so they had to go to another room.

After we finished eating, our grandpa would sometimes say, "You kids want to hear a good story?" Of course we would all say, "Yeah." He would get his smoking pipe out of his bib overalls then get the tobacco sack out, fill his pipe, and pack it down with his thumb. Then the matches came out of another pocket and he would take a match out of the box then close it and just sit there looking at us. We could hardly wait for him to start, but for me I was always thinking, *Will he forget and light his pipe?* I would watch him and then look at our mom. She did not pay any attention to that as she knew he would not do such a thing. Yet I was thinking, *What if?*

Our parents had heard all of his stories a number of times, but never left the table while he was telling one of his stories to us kids. He would back his chair away from the table, turn sideways, look back at us kids, and start the story. "The double-S mountain road," he said, "was just barely a road, yet it was well-traveled. It was as crooked as a snake," he would say. Back then, only a few families lived near that road. It was hilly with lots of curves; trees and brush covered both side of the roads. It was a lonesome and wild area, and at the bottom was a stream. A small creek ran across the road. My grandpa said it was a steady stream, meaning that it ran all the time. He said it was just like the one us kids went swimming in…just like it. Here my grandpa would start setting the story up, with that look and changing his tone of voice.

The county was wild back then; you had to be mighty careful. He said you'd never know what kind of man or animal you would meet out on that old crooked road. He then would give us that stern look and pause. He said he was just a young man back then but, as time went on; a few sad-looking houses were being built just off that old road. "Strangers were moving in, folks that we did not know. They looked like men that you couldn't trust. Could they be running from the law?" He would say it seemed to him like there were always stories and things happening along this mountain road that just didn't seem right. "And," he would say with a slow, low voice, "that seemed like a bad-luck crooked country road."

One time a neighbor's horse was attacked by a wild cat and as the fellow was trying to save his horse, the cat attacked him. My grandpa said that for the rest of his life he was a sorry sight to look at as the cat scarred him for life; part of his face was missing. (Conley turned and looked at me as to make sure that I had both sides of my face.) He said he could never figure out how this fellow ever lived. It seemed like all the bad things that were happening along this road were at or near the stream that ran across the road at the bottom of this mountain. He would tell about other happenings he had seen or heard about. He said a horse thief was hung from an old oak tree along that road; they cut him down and buried him on the spot. He told us one time he saw the largest, blackest snake he had ever seen just where the creek crossed the road. He would then start drawing a picture for us, twisting his arms and body and trying to make the hissing sound that the snake made as it was all curled up right there in the middle of the road. He then rolled his eyes at each of us kids sitting around the table, and then he would say, kind of slowly, that it could have easily swallowed a dog. Conley looked at me with that look as if to say, "Why did he have to tell us that?" I was too scared to say anything. I looked at my mom and she acted as if she didn't even hear it. I am guessing that she had heard all these stories a number of times.

He went on. We knew it was going to get scarier. He said from where he lived way back then, this road became a shortcut to one of his friends' place. He and this fellow would swap work, help each other cut wood, and, later on, my grandpa helped him build a four-stall hip-roof barn. It was during this time that new folks were moving in and some of them seemed suspicious. Some were loners, others were from other counties and were thought to have been running from the law or who knows what. Back then most people kept to themselves and asked very few questions; it was best just to leave some folks alone.

Later on, a wedding was planned. A young widowed lady was to be married to a fellow that lived off this road a few miles. Most of the time back then, when people got married, they just went to the preacher's house and in a few minutes, and with a few dollars, it was over. Kinda simple. (That's how our mom and dad went about this.) As the story goes on, it appears that this lady wanted a bit more than a two-dollar wedding. It was planned and people were invited. A home wedding was something special back then. My grandpa was invited as he knew the brother of the groom, the fellow who he helped build the hip-roof barn. It was to be outside in the yard. Food was prepared. Everyone came who was invited, the preacher and everyone, except the bride. Where was the bride?

The people who had gathered were watching and anticipating the bride coming down the road in a one-horse buggy. She was late. Hours went by. The folks were talking. Had she changed her mind, was she having second thoughts? Was she was backing out? There was a stirring about all this. This situation was unsettling and a sense of gloom was in the air. My grandpa said something was wrong. Folks who knew her said she was not the type to just back out. It was now starting to get late and some of the people were leaving. My grandpa, the groom, and his brother hitched two horses to an old wagon and set out to see if they could find her. He looked at us kids and said, "Wonder what happened to the bride?" As if we would know.

They went one way and found nothing then down a different road and, again, nothing.

By then it was almost dark as they drove the team along the rough and rocky road down to where the stream crossed that old crooked road. He said he had a bad feeling about this, and, sure enough, as they approached the bottom of the hill, an eerie feeling came upon all of them, even the two horses. The team stopped and they could not be forced to go any farther. Down by the creek, they could see the buggy. The bride and her horse were missing; her buggy was a mess as it was wrapped around a tree. The team was acting up and now was uncontrollable. Something was dreadfully wrong there; horses have that sense about them and, for the most part, are easily spooked. And they had a good reason to be, for what they saw was not the least bit encouraging. Part of her dress had been ripped from her and was now waving in the breeze from a small bush along the road. "And it was blood red," he said…blood red. He would wave his hands as if to show us the breeze blowing that ripped her dress.

The search went on through the night and for a number of weeks following the incident. Nothing more was found except the horse and it was horrible-looking. My grandpa said, "Where did she go? What happened? Did she just vanish into thin air? How can a person do that?" He looked at us as if we had the answer.

I looked at my sister across the table. She had stopped eating and now looked with that blank stare and her mouth was half-open and she did not blink. Maybe she was looking at me with my mouth and my eyes wide open. Conley was as stiff as a board; all of us were taken in by all of this. When my grandpa told these stories, I would become mesmerized and it seemed like I was there in that moment with him. He could pull you in with how he told the story. It seemed like I was there at that small stream at the bottom of that scary place, seeing everything in my own mind just as he described it. He made them seem so real and our dad, with a few words, added to the story; that made it seem even more so that this story was real. There was no doubt this was a real event that he remembered back about fifty years are more when he was a young man.

Anyway, back to the story. He said that this road, from that point on, was hardly ever traveled at night, especially with a team. And, from time to time, a fellow could be seen walking because his horse had bucked him off and had run away at or near the place where her buggy was found. There was no way you could get a team or a horse to cross the small stream. They would become so spooked and uncontrollable, it was just no use trying. (I know from experience that a horse or mule, when spooked, is impossible to control. They will run, kick, and even die trying to escape the danger or perceived danger.)

"Now here is the scary part," my grandpa would say. From time to time in the evening, a lady with a red wedding dress could be seen crossing the road at that exact place where she disappeared. She would appear and cross the road with a loud terrifying scream, the sound made the hair stand up on the back of your neck as she faded away into the night air.

My grandpa said he did not have the nerve to take that road, even in the daytime. But he had talked to eyewitnesses who, late in the evening, saw a lady crossing the road at the bottom of that hill and disappear wearing that long red dress; her scream would echo down the mountain as she vanished into the woods. One person said she stopped in the middle of the road and then disappeared right before his eyes…and her scream made his blood run cold as it was the most terrifying sound he had ever heard.

Then he finished talking. He just sat there; everyone was quiet. Later he would be talking to himself, in a low voice: "It was red. No one ever wears a red dress to a wedding. It was...blood red." He looked around, tapped the tobacco in his pipe, the match was out of the box, he was ready to get up and go smoke. He started to get up from the table.

Then he said, "Oh, I almost forgot the last part. The fellow who she was going to marry, the groom, over the weeks just about went crazy thinking what might have happened to her. Someone said he went to the very spot where she had disappeared and waited for her to come by. From that time on no one knew what happened to him. He was never seen again. No one ever lived in his old house. It just rotted down. Yet some said, from time to time, there was a lantern light in the bedroom. Did he go to the bottom of that old mountain and wait for her? Did she take him away? Are there now two ghosts living in the mountain air alongside that crooked road…or did they move into that old house?"

He would look at all of us and I think I could see a twinkle in his eyes and the look on his face that told me he had presented a good story. Again, he would slide his chair back and give us one more look as he thanked my mom for a good meal; then he walked slowly to the living room to smoke his pipe. At times I thought I could hear him chuckling to himself.

Now it was close to our bed time. Mom said for us boys to get up from the table and go outside to the bathroom before we went to bed. Conley said he did not have to go. I said, "Oh, yes, you do." I was not going out into the dark by myself.

I thought to myself, *Blood red*.

18

MOHAWKS AND CREW CUTS

Someone said, "Did you see Hugh Marlin's haircut this morning?" I could not believe what I was seeing. It was the most talked about thing in our country school for at least a few days. He had a mohawk. Hugh Marlin was a different breed, kind of a wild kid, and he was in his glory being the center of attention. I think most of us were wondering what Mr. Ryan, the principal, would do. Would he send him home? Would he be called into his office for a good talking to? A mohawk…it was the first time I had ever seen someone with a mohawk haircut. Mr. Ryan, of course, did not pay any attention and that was the right thing to do, especially with Hugh Marlin.

I think from the beginning of time until this very day, the way we wore, cut, and shaped our hair has been one of the most important factors of our lives. Each generation, from as far back as there is a recorded history, did it their way. Yet when I saw the mohawk, it was so interesting to me. I was for sure not going to have my head look like that. Of course, the mohawk is still around and again it is interesting to see.

Getting a good haircut was so important to me—always has been. As a young kid, I did not have a choice; my parents would take us to the barber shop and tell the barber how to cut it. That was it. But that all changed when I became a teenager. I for sure wanted to fit into the crowd. I wanted to be pretty much like the rest of the boys in my class. Back in the 1950s, I do not remember any of the boys with long hair nor did anyone have his head shaved. I think that would have been the worst of the worst.

I just wanted to pretty much blend in with the crowd, did not want to stand out. I just wanted to be one of the guys. I combed my short hair, used Red Rose hair oil, and tried to look as good as I could. In 1954, I turned fourteen years old and was now on the Ryan High School basketball team. My hair was always a mess after practice. Our coach had a crew cut; most of the players had a crew cut. My friend J.C. told me after practice that it was good to have me on the team but if I was going to be a basketball player, I needed to look like one. I had to think about that.

Later I told my mom that I was going to get a crew cut. She said, "No, you're not." I said I wanted to look like the rest of the guys. She said, "If they all dyed their hair blue, would you want to do that?" I said, "Yes." She turned around and stared at me. I said, "I'm just kidding."

Mr. John Ellenburg cut my hair most of the time. I stopped at his house and asked if he could give me a crew cut and how much that would cost. He said, "It would be twice as much as a regular haircut." That meant that I had to come up with fifty cents. That was a lot of money for a haircut. I then asked just for the heck of it, "How much for a mohawk?" He looked at me and started laughing and said, "A hundred dollars. You would really be a sight to see with a hair cut like that." I think he knew I was kidding about the mohawk.

What would my family think if I came home with a crew cut? Hey, I was now a teenager and could do whatever I wanted to with myself and, more so, my hair. Well, that was my thinking back then. But down deep inside I knew it would never happen until I could convince my mom of that idea. My thinking was that I had to take little steps. So the next time I asked Mr. John to cut it shorter than usual and see how that would go over. He did a good job; it was pretty darn short. The only thing wrong with really short hair was that it made me look like a kid. Gosh, I didn't want that. I wanted to look more grown up…I was tired of being a kid.

One more problem with short hair, and it was a major one for me. I had a darn cowlick and it took a lot of hair grease to make it look normal. Well, anyway, no one said anything about my haircut. From time to time, I would comb it straight up in front to see how it would look. So far, so good.

A few months later, I finally got up the nerve to ask Mr. John to give me a crew cut. We went out on the front porch and he said, "Are you sure?" I said, "Yep." Ten minutes later, I gave him fifty cents. He looked at me and then at the two quarters and then gave me one back. Twenty-five cents for a crew cut. What a deal!

Now I went back home and was just trying to act normal, like nothing had changed. But as most of us know, you can never pull anything over on your mom. I was walking on thin ice, wearing my old cap most of the time and hoping that she would not come unglued the first time she noticed. Sometimes it is best just to get right to the heart of things, so I walked in the kitchen without my cap on. She was starting a fire in the cook stove. I asked her if she needed more wood. She looked at me then turned around and said if she did, she would go get it herself. I knew by her answer that she did not approve. As I was leaving the room, I thought she said something like…I was a sorry-looking thing. I wonder what she would have said if I had come home with a mohawk.

I loved playing basketball, loved the way my hair looked, and it was so much easier to take care of. I wore a crew cut for a year or so. I do not think my mom ever got used to it. She said it was wrong for boys to have their hair sticking straight up. None of my brothers ever had a crew cut and for sure none ever had a mohawk. I am guessing that they did not want to butt heads with our Mom.

19

THE OUTHOUSE

If I had to choose just one thing from all the inventions of our times, it would be the wonderful modern bathroom that we take for granted today.

All the outhouses that I have visited over my lifetime were all different, some in small ways, and some were pretty darn nice…that is, compared to the worst ones. On Rural Route One, I believe every farm house had an outhouse. Our church had two outhouses, one for men and one for women. Our elementary school had two outhouses. The boys had five stalls and a good-sized pee area. I grew up thinking nothing about all that. It was just the way it was and, for the most part, I didn't know any different. Life was good.

Those old outhouses, if well cared for, were so much better than most of today's so-called modern port-a-potties. Of course, both serve a very important part in our lives, for sure. I remember us taking some cotton and soaking it with vanilla extract and hanging that by a string to cover up some of the smell, and it worked pretty darn good for a week or so. But the best thing ever for the old "john" was a bucket of lime. A well-kept, nice, clean outhouse was hard to find.

The thirtieth president of the United States, President Calvin Coolidge, had an outhouse with a window. That wouldn't have worked on our farm. Can you believe that people sign up for outhouse tours? Not me—never in a million years. And there is a real outhouse wall of fame. I don't know what to say about that. A song by Billy Ed Wheeler is titled, "The Little Brown Shack out Back." Yes,

I can believe that might go over pretty good in some areas of our country. Charles Sale wrote a book about outhouses, *The Specialist*, that sold over a million copies. Can you believe that?

Today we can laugh about, make fun of, and be thankful that those days are pretty much gone and the old outhouse is just a thing of the past…thank goodness. Yet, when there is one on display at a county fair or some early pioneer village, it is the one place where some folks want to sit down inside and have their picture taken. Not me.

Thinking back over the years of my youth, we had some sorry-looking, smelly, and shabby outhouses, but the one by where we lived in the hollow was one of the better buildings on our rented farm. It had a cement floor; it had vents, and a real store-bought seat. Of all the buildings on our farm, that brown shack out back made us all thought that we were doing pretty darn good.

Keeping the old john clean was not a bad job and, for the most part, I did not mind that chore. I made sure there was an outdated Sears and Roebuck catalog, plenty of old *Decatur Daily* newspapers, and a couple of the *Progressive Farmers* magazines. There had to be plenty of reading material stacked on a small shelf, usually a comic book like Roy Rogers or Gene Autry. Once or twice a month, I would take a bucket of lye soap and give it a quick scrub down. Sometimes I would fill a mason jar with wild honeysuckles or lilacs when they were blooming. Fresh pine needles and some cedar chips made a big difference also. But, most of all, using plenty of lime was the secret to keeping the outhouse presentable.

The only problem with our family was that there was only one outhouse for us five kids and our parents. One of my sisters (she knows who she is) would go out there and just sit, and sometimes sing, for the longest time. We had to throw a rock or something at the building to get her out.

In our kitchen was a table where the water bucket and the wash pan set. The dipper and flour sack towel hung on a nail. Each time we came in the back door, our mom made us wash our hands. Even if we had not been to the outhouse, she would always say, "Wash your hands anyway."

It was always interesting when you went to someone's home and you went to their outhouse; it was never the same as ours. It seemed like ours smelled better. Or maybe it was just what you got used to.

I think this is a good place to stop as my mind is wandering back to those yesterday years. Hmmmmmm…what is that smell?

20

PICKING COTTON

Of all the jobs I have had in life, none of them were as hard or as bad as picking cotton by hand. To me, this is the worst of all the jobs on or off the farm. If you could walk or crawl, you could pick cotton. It took absolutely no skills whatsoever. For the rest of my life, whenever I thought I was being overworked or had a bad job, even in Viet Nam, I would think that it was much better than picking cotton. I am just thinking here: what if I had been born in the mid-'60s? John Deere would have had the cotton picker, but that is the way it goes. We were the cotton pickers.

All of us started picking cotton before we started school. Even if you only picked five pounds, that would help. I remember my little sister Juanita, at four years old, with a toe sack picking alongside my dad. All of us were involved in this back-breaking chore. It made your fingers bleed, your back and shoulders hurt, and if you crawled on your knees, they would hurt also. Picking cotton by hand is a back-breaking, no-skill, hard way to make a dollar, plain and simple.

The pick sack had a shoulder strap that you used to pull the sack along. Most of them had a coat of tar on the bottom side to keep the sack from wearing out as you dragged it along the ground. The pick sacks were of different length, from four feet to seven feet...maybe some even longer. As we got older, the sacks we used got longer. I usually picked two rows at a time, the rest only one. This was to keep all of us in line, but more so for Dad to keep an eye on all of us. Lena Elizabeth loved to watch the birds fly over; I loved to watch the airplanes and wish that I was the pilot of each one. I can remember watching and daydreaming and then, out of nowhere, a cotton limb would be used on my backside. That took care of the pilot's job; I crashed.

Just a little note here; sometimes when one of my brothers or sisters was looking at the birds or clouds and our dad was not looking, I would throw something at them and then really start picking cotton as if I had no idea what was going on. It would scare the heck out of them; they thought that our dad was the one doing the throwing. I thought that was so funny.

If the dew was heavy, the cotton weighed more, so in the morning it seemed like you could pick more than in the afternoon. A seven-foot cotton sack packed full would weigh around sixty-five pounds. How long the rows were and how good the cotton was determined how far you could pick until your sack was full. When it was full, you had to somehow get it on your shoulders and carry it back to the wagon to weigh. The first person to get their pick sack full determined when we stopped picking and went to the wagon to weigh. Most of the time, Conley and I had to go and carry our sisters' pick sacks to the wagon.

The wagon was used for almost everything on the farm, from hauling manure to riding us to church, to the store, and so on. During cotton-picking time, the side boards were installed and were at least eight feet high.

Each sack was weighed and the number of pounds written down in the book by each name. Our dad did all the weighing. Then somehow it had to be lifted up the side of the wagon and the sack emptied. Conley and I did that job. Then we would walk around and pack it down. At the end of the day, our dad would tally what each one of us picked and, if we were slacking off, we would get a talking to. Of course, he already knew before then. Also, each day the total that we all picked would be added to the list. We needed around twelve hundred pounds (if it was picked heavy, with lots of morning dew, we would need at least fourteen hundred pounds) on the wagon before it was taken to the gin. With all the seeds removed, that would make a five-hundred-pound bale, the average weight. I think it was better to have the bale weigh a little over five hundred than to have it under five hundred.

We used two different types of scales. One was just a plain, spring-type scale; the other was a weight-and-balance type, and it had been around for a long, long time, yet it was very accurate. I think one was used to make sure the other was weighing the correct amount.

How many pounds could a person pick in one day depended on how good the cotton was and how hard you wanted to work. I have heard stories of guys picking well over four hundred pounds per day. One time I heard of a younger guy who lived just up the road from us picking five hundred pounds; that had to be a really long day and some very good cotton. At two dollars per hundred, he was making some good money back in the 1950s. On average, when I was about sixteen years old, I could pick 350 and if it was really good cotton 400 pounds a day.

We all went to the field when it was cotton-picking time. Our whole family, our dad plus six kids, even our mom, would help in the afternoon. Juanita, at three and four years old, would take care of little Rachel at the end of the rows by the wagon. Of course, we all kept a close eye out for them. I always thought it was something that our mom came and helped us...as if she did not have enough to do. On a good day, when the cotton was good, all of us could pick a bale per day. Now, this would be a very good day picking.

The next day someone, usually me, had to take all of this to the gin. While the wagon was gone, everyone picked until their pick sacks were full, and then waited for the wagon to return. Generally speaking, we could pick four bales per week and that was only if the cotton was good. During the last few years that I was home, we farmed around fifteen acres of cotton, about the same in corn and hay. Forty-five acres is a lot when using only two mules and doing all the labor by hand. As you can see, we had plenty of hard labor to do.

A very good year and a good farmer with good land could average about a bale per acre. I don't think we ever achieved that goal. We usually had to pick a second time. I remember once going back again for the third time to try to get just a little bit more, which was the pits. I pretty much knew early in my life that farming was not for me...at least this kind of farming. It was so very hard for anyone to get ahead with this type of set-up. Of course, we were sharecroppers.

At times, we hired out to help other farmers pick cotton. We would walk five miles and pick cotton all day long then walk back home. This sounds like it was hard work...and it was. Yet we did it without complaining. I guess we knew that we were making money and that was a good thing.

I've heard a few people say that they loved picking cotton; I could not believe they used the word "love" in conjunction with picking cotton, but maybe they did. I am sure they just enjoyed being out in the cotton patch. Some people would pick side by side and talk all day as they pulled that pick sack across the field and back again. My little sister Fran, at an early age, fell in love with a young kid while picking cotton side by side. She and Johnny have been married for more than fifty years. She could not have *picked* a better guy. Finding romance in the cotton patch...now that makes picking cotton a little better!

So here I will just smile and be thankful for the memories and thank God I do not have to do that anymore. Over the years, I have learned it is a good thing to enjoy your vocation and, if you do, then you will never work another day in your life.

But, for me, I never found a hoe that would fit my hands...or a pick sack that was just the right color.

21

FIRST DATE—A KISS
AND A MISS

She was the most stunning girl I had ever seen, standing there on the front porch of their rural country home waiting for me. Her beauty was glowing as she introduced me to her mom, who was also very pretty. I have always heard that if the mother is good-looking then the daughter will grow up and be even more beautiful. This was just too good to be true. Their dog was so happy to see me and was jumping up on me and wanting to be petted; now my clean blue jeans had red dirt on the front, yet so far, so good. My first date...I was all smiles.

Almost sixteen years old, well on my way to manhood, and up until then I had never...I mean never been on a date. Most of my classmates had gone to the movies or the drive-in soda places on a date in Hartselle or Arab. But not me. I had not even held hands with a lady. First, I had no transportation and also...no money. I was beginning to think that I would grow old and never have been on a date. Fifteen years of my life gone. Halfway through my teenage years, and not even a girlfriend.

Our small country school I think had more boys than girls. I was not one of the lucky guys who had a girlfriend. I knew that my status as a teenager was not as good as I would have liked. Yet I knew me, knew that if I would have had the right clothes, I could dress up pretty good. For now it was blue jeans, a cotton shirt, and a pair of work shoes that were well worn and almost too small.

For the most part, I was not "one of the guys" in our small school. I would have never been elected to any office in our class, was not a star at any sports, nor was I a stand-out in any subject. Just a regular kid trying to fit in where I could. Back then girls would have never asked a guy for a date, and, for sure, none of them would have ever asked me, and not one of them would have ever given me the eye. There were some really pretty ladies going to our country school at Ryan. I do not think I had the nerve to even ask any of them out for a date. Though I had five sisters, I was dumber than a rock when it came to girls.

Some of the guys would brag about how many times they had been out on a date and how much fun they had when they went to the movies or just riding around. I would listen to them and day-dream—daydream about sitting close to a beautiful young lady with pretty hair, her smelling good, holding hands, and just talking. I started thinking, *What if? What if I got a date and what would it be like? What if I really liked her; what would I do or say? What if she liked me—how would I react? What if she did not like me? What if…what if…and what if?* My voice was now changing from squeaky to a more grown-up-boy type. Yet, when I got excited, what I wanted to say and what I did say did not sound very manly at all.

Here I must give credit to a friend of mine who was now enrolled in our school and was in the same grade with me. Without him, this would never have come about. Jay was a real country boy. He would have been a great advertisement for the Country Gentleman Tobacco Company. He loved to smoke, but not the ready-rolled kind of cigarettes. He rolled his own and he was good at it. He would take the OCB cigarette paper out and fill it with his Country Gentleman Tobacco. To close the tobacco sack, he would take one of the strings by his teeth and pull the strings tight then put it back into his shirt pocket. Then with his fingers, he would roll it up, give it a lick, and, boy, did it ever look as neat as a Camel! Now with it in his mouth, he would take a match and light it as if he were the real Marlboro man. He took pride in his homemade cigarettes and he made smoking look good…as if that could ever be.

Jay kept the small tobacco sack in his shirt pocket, but he always let the strings that tied the tobacco sack hang out so everyone could see. He took pride in all that. He thought he was a class act...and in some ways he was. I had a lot of fun hanging out with him; he was a good guy.

He was always telling me that we needed to find us some girl-friends. Heck, I was all for that. I said, "What if we did? What would we do?" He looked at me then shook his head like I didn't know any-thing...well; he was about half-right. He said, "We would take them to a movie, go get something to eat at a drive-in, or just ride around."

His parents had a 1949 black four-door Ford. Jay was a year older than I was so he had his driver's license and his dad would let him drive it as long as he was back home by 10:00 p.m.

Jay was now really into this girlfriend thing. He was now on the prowl. He was looking. He just had to be like everyone else and have his very own girlfriend. And, lo and behold, he met a very pretty little girl who was sixteen. She was easy to talk to, had a ready-made smile...she was just perfect for Jay. He met her when we (Ryan High School) were playing at Cotaco High School at one of our basketball games. Now here is the good part: this lady he met had a friend who saw me play basketball and all she knew about me was that I wore the number 12 on my basketball jersey. Later, Jay told me that she wanted to go on a date with me. When Jay told me this, I could not believe it! I was very excited, to say the least.

I was now entering into a new stage in life: the dating game. Everyone in my class knew that I had a date; how they knew, I do not know. Maybe it was the big ole smile all the way across my face, or maybe it was the grapevine. Of course, there were no secrets in our small country school or the community.

I have always been good at daydreaming, but now this was dif-ferent. It was consuming my mind and my thinking. My first date.

I wanted to make sure that my parents would let me go so I had to tell my mom and also had to see if my dad would let me have a couple of dollars for the great event. He would always wait until the last minute to say "yes" or "no." He thought it was a waste of money and, at fifteen years old, I was too young to be out that late at night (9:00 p.m.) on such a thing as a date. I was starting to worry.

Jay was now the man. I hung on to every word as we talked about all this. I had tons of questions and he was getting tired of me being so inquisitive…hey, this was a first for me! I wanted all the information. I wanted to know everything about holding hands, talking, what to say, what not to say. Should I do this or that? Do I sit close to her? And, most of all, do I kiss her…do I kiss her on the first date? Jay said, "Don't worry, it will be okay; everything will come natural. Just be yourself." Yeah, right. I was already a mess. The daydreaming stuff was getting to be way too much. I needed really good instructions, an "Everything You Will Ever Need to Know about Dating" pamphlet or a book about dating for dummies.

Our teachers were always telling us that to do well on a test you had to pay attention in class and do lots of studying; homework was a must. Coach Ralph was always telling us that to be good at basketball you had to practice, practice, and practice. Now I was thinking all about that. I needed help, and how in the world could I practice? I would not dare ask anyone in my class, not in a hundred years. I would have loved to have been the driver for some of my classmates as they went out on a date or a mouse in the car just to witness the event, but that was not to be. I guess it was like swimming; just jump in the water and either you swim or drown. I was now beginning to sweat.

Getting ready for this thing was getting to me. First, I needed a haircut. I was sporting a crew cut and, for the most part, I thought I looked like a twelve-year-old. I needed to look older, more grown up. So about three days before the big event, I started trying to comb my hair down. I wanted to be sure I had just the right shirt…I only had two. Blue jeans without a belt and a short-sleeve shirt would be my attire. My old shoes would have to do. Like it or not, that was all I had. Now, to make everything look good. I needed to make sure they were clean and to starch and iron them with a sharp crease. I did not have to be told that first impressions meant a lot.

There were a few more days to go and now my mom was asking me all kinds of questions. "Who is this girl?"

I said, "She is a young lady that goes to school at Plainview."

"What is her name?"

"Kathryn."

"Where does she live?"

"On a farm close to my friend Jay."

My sisters were also asking all kinds questions. "Is she pretty?" "What color hair? Is it long or short?" "Does she have freckles?" Gosh, they had to know everything!

Jay said we were good to go on Friday night and that he would pick me up and for me to be ready as we did not want to be late. I was getting butterflies in my stomach. This was not a daydream; it was the real thing. After school I had to get all my chores done, get cleaned up, and be ready when he arrived.

At the last minute I almost forgot that I needed some money. I had a dollar or so change but that would not be enough. My mom came to my rescue with her egg money and gave me two dollars. I was good to go.

Here came Jay in a cloud of dust, driving right up into our yard. I climbed in and noticed that he was smoking one of his roll-your-own cigarettes. He looked cool and much more grown up than I did. Well, anyway, it was what it was. My first date.

It was about 6:00 p.m. My hands were sweating, yet I was so excited as we drove up into their yard and there she was, talking to her mom on their front porch. Now to get out of the car without falling or tripping over my feet as I walked as manly as I could up to the porch and up the steps. I was wishing I had a voice like Johnny Cash so I could just say, "Hello, my name is Will McCollum and do you ever look beautiful." But I sounded more like June Carter. Her mom gave me the once-over look then told me to take care of her daughter and make sure she was back by nine. She asked if I had watch. Heck, no, and neither did Jay. Now I was thinking if she was five minutes late that I might be in a lot of trouble. More sweat.

I assured her mom that I would have her back by nine. I wiped the sweat off my hands and escorted her to the car as Jay and his girlfriend were watching my every step. I opened the door; she climbed in. I closed the door, walked around to the other side, and got in. There she was, looking so beautiful. I was smiling…really smiling. Then Jay looked back at me and said her door was not closed. What?

Now I went back out and did it all over again. I tried to say something funny…or at least I thought it was funny. I was still smiling…I think.

Jay backed out and we headed down the dusty country road out to the main highway then into town. Hartselle, Alabama, was the place to go. The best drive-in root beer stand ever was on Highway 31. Jay drove in like he owned the place. A teenage girl who worked there as a car hop came to our car and all of us ordered a root beer float. Jay and his girlfriend were good talkers and that made it easier for me. All I had to do was just sit there and smile. By then I was getting good at the smiling thing. I was not sure if my voice would fail me and go squeaky if I spoke. So many things were going through my mind. First, I did not want to spill my root beer and I was just trying to look cool.

We were now ready to go for a drive. Jay backed out and stopped. He looked around then asked if we cared if he smoked. What could we say? He got the cigarette paper out then his Country Gentleman Tobacco and rolled the best-looking cigarette ever. We watched and he knew we were watching. Again, he made smoking look good. Away we went down Highway 31 toward Decatur. We were cruising, just talking with all the windows down—what a really nice ride. Jay was smoking, driving, and talking like he was the man. About two miles down the road, he flipped what was left of his homemade cigarette out the window.

As we entered the city of Decatur, we stopped at the entryway to a drive-in movie to see what was playing and thinking that the next time—if there was a next time—we would come back and see a movie. All at once I felt something hot on my neck. I looked down and, believe it or not, I was smoking! I thought, *what the heck is going on?* I had to get out of the car fast and get my shirt off because Jay's cigarette—or what was left of it—had come back through the open window, landed on me, and was burning a hole in my good shirt. There I stood with my shirt off, putting out the fire. Jay felt bad, I felt worse, and Kathryn was looking at my bony chest. She came to my rescue, helping to make sure the fire was out and with getting my shirt back on. She said while holding my hand, "I am so glad that you don't smoke." Now I was smiling again.

The rest of the evening went pretty well. We held hands and I was now in the conversation, talking when I could get a word in. Later, they all thought the burned hole in my shirt was funny… except Jay had to say that he was glad the cigarette landed on me and not on the seat since he would have had to explain all that to his dad. I thought, *WHAT?*

The time was going so fast; it seemed like we were just getting started. But we had to head back so Kathryn could be home by nine. We drove up the driveway to her home, stopped, and talked for a minute or two. I got out and went around, opened her door, and walked her to the front porch. Here came the decision: *do I kiss her goodnight or what?* I was thinking just a peck on her cheek would be okay. I walked her up the steps and told her I had a good time; she smiled and said she did, too. She said I had a hole in my shirt and we both laughed. I thought a little kiss on her forehead would do no harm. Everything this whole evening was a first for me. Now the first kiss…

I had noticed when I got a chance to see a movie or a show on TV that, when the couple kissed, both had their eyes closed. So I thought if I did kiss her, I would know *that,* at least. I looked at her; she had a little smile. So I leaned over, closed my eyes, and kissed her on the side of her face. Hey…that felt so good—not bad for the first time. She just stood there like maybe she wanted one more. Again I leaned toward her, lined up for one more kiss, closed my eyes, and, to my complete surprise, I missed and kissed her right smack on her left eye! She backed away and looked at me funny, as I must have had the dumbest look on my face and was looking like an idiot, thinking, *what in the world have I done?* How in the world could I have missed? She said, "Goodnight." I just looked at her as she left me standing there on her front porch.

My life was now over.

I walked back and climbed in the car. Jay asked me, "Did you kiss her?"

"Yes."

"Was it good?"

"Yes."

"Tell me more," he said.

Here you will have to read between the lines as my reputation was now on the line. I said, "Jay, it was the best kiss I have ever had."

He said, "Really?! Tell me more, Will."

I said, "Jay that is all you need to know."

I was pulled between being upchucking sick and trying to put on the best front ever. Jay and I talked as we headed back to the hollow where I lived. I gave him a dollar for gas and, for the most part, was so glad to be back home. It was my very first experience with dating.

My first-ever date: a kiss…and a miss.

P.S. Kathryn and I became good friends; we wrote to each other often for about a year or so. I had to take life as it came. First, I had no money. I was way young, there was so much work there on the farm, and we lived about fifteen miles apart. I would ride my old bicycle down to see here a number of times. She really was a very pretty lady. I joined the army; she went to college. She later married a nice guy who lived just down the road from her. Life usually turns out pretty good if you just hang in there.

22

THE PEDDLER

The peddler bus came by our house every Tuesday, and what a great day it was. It was an old type of a vehicle...could have been an old school bus. It was painted up and when you saw it coming down the road, it made us all smile. When we had a chance to be home during the time the peddler came, it was something. As he drove to our house, he would be blowing the horn and we knew it was him. All of us kids would run to the front porch and wait to watch him pull into our yard. It was like Christmas every week.

This peddler had everything you could ever dream of: stuff was hanging on the walls, in boxes, on the shelves—there were even chickens in a coop on the back and on top of the bus. He would buy eggs, buy chickens, and then go down the road and sell them to other folks. The smell inside was intoxicating (you have read that I use the word "smell" a lot...I am still using it); I could not get enough of this. I was always the last one to get back out when my mom was finished.

It was a thrill to be home when he came and most of the time Mom would let us go inside this bus with her. I can't tell you how much I enjoyed this. I wished for the fancy-colored sunglasses, pocket knives that had pictures of Roy Rogers on the handles, a cap with something written on the front. I remember my sister Fran touching every item that she could reach, like she was thinking to herself, *I want one of these*. I think all of us wanted one.

My mom did not charge anything; if she did not have the money or couldn't sell eggs, she didn't buy anything. She only used cash... always. Yet when she was a nickel short, the driver would say, "Oh, don't worry about that; you can pay me next time." One time he asked my mom how many kids she had. She said way too many and more than she could afford. He thought that was so funny and then he tried to give her ten cents' worth of bubble gum for us kids. She said, "No, they don't need any of that." I think he felt kinda disappointed…..we were, too.

She would sell eggs to him then use that money to buy what she needed. My mom was always looking for a bargain. She wanted to know if he had an old hen he would sell to her cheap as she wanted to make chicken and dumplings for a Sunday dinner. He said, "Yes." There was one on top that she could have for fifty cents. She said she would take it. We all moved out of the way and watched as he climbed up on top to get the old hen out of the chicken coop. As he was climbing back down, the hen got away from him and ran under our house. Our mom looked at him, still holding on to her fifty cents. He said, "Guess she was not as old as I thought." He climbed back up and got another one. I don't remember how they settled up.

We had a small gallon can with a spout on it and, from time to time, when we needed coal oil (kerosene), he would fill it for us then stick a potato on the spout so it wouldn't spill. I thought that was a great idea. He treated all of us very fair and loved to show us kid's new things…of course, it made us want one. Mom would start backing us out as she knew we could easily be tempted.

He drove all over the country and was a really wonderful person to do business with, and his prices were not much different from the general store. Those were the best of days.

The Watkins man

The Watkins man came every month or so also. It was like the drug store came to our house; we were all gathered around looking at all the stuff he had. He sold salve, soap, liniment, pills, and everything that you might need for the house and for all kinds of ailments. Even items for the livestock. I remember Mom buying lotions that healed all kinds of injuries and sores for us kids and for the livestock. Blue Gaul lotion was one of the best. It was purple, a real dark purple. It really worked and was used a lot on the cows and horses...and on us, too. If it helped heal a sore on the mule, it surely would heal a sore on your foot. I can remember using it where it would not show on my legs and feet. This blue lotion, once applied to the wound, was there for a long time. You could not wash it off; you had to wear it off.

The Watkins man would have a couple of suitcase-type displays. Of course, he was a salesman and what he sold he swore would help heal every kind of ailment you could think of. Mom usually purchased some salve and was pretty good at saying no...Of course, we could only buy if we had the money. The Watkins produce was good and I still see it on the store shelves at some drug stores today.

Four dollars and twenty-five cents for the insurance man

The insurance man came to our house once a month to collect the premiums. He usually wore a shirt and tie; he looked like a doctor. He was invited in and Mom or Dad would scrape up enough nickels and dimes to make the premium payment. Our parents carried life insurance on all of us until we left home; it was more or less burial insurance.

This fellow had a really large leather case that had all of the information in reference to our insurance policies. He would look through until he found the name and would say, "You owe this much." It seemed like it took all the money we had just to keep those policies paid up. Sometimes he would ask one of us kids if we wanted to see our name on his list. Oh, yes we wanted to see. Then he would unfold that big leather binder and...there it was: our name in print.

He was never in a hurry, always loved to sit and talk. You could tell he liked what he was doing. He was not a salesman to us; he was a friend of our family. There were times when we did not have enough money for all the premiums. He would take money from his pocket and said it was now paid in full. Our dad kept track of what he owed and, later, the differences were paid to him. I will never forget how we had to save the nickels and dimes and every penny to make sure that there was enough money for the insurance man.

It seemed like he came at around eleven-thirty or twelve—dinnertime—and my mom would invite him to stay for dinner, the noon meal. Sometimes he did. At that time, I thought it would be a great job: being all dressed up, looking good, selling insurance, and collecting those nickels and dimes. But more so being there for people when they most needed help.

23

NEIGHBORS

How can I get away without words of thanks to the many people who, not knowing it, made a big impression on me as I grew up? Some of them are old friends who remain so 'til this day; some were wonderful neighbors with words of encouragement that I most surely needed; and some were just good folks passing by.

And since determination is fueled as much by doubters as by supporters, let me also thank those who said that I didn't have a chance.

—--

The Ellenburgs were our closest neighbors, and what a great family. They lived just up the hill from us. Mr. John, Mrs. Louie, and their children: Billy Wayne, Martha Gale, John Jr. (we called him Pete), Cicero, Jerry, and Kenneth. We could not have had a more wonderful family living that close to us.

Mr. John cut my hair so many times when I had no money to pay him. He was a no-nonsense type of a guy. What he said is what he meant. If I got out of line, he had no problems setting me straight… and I knew that. I knew he liked me because a number of times he would tell me how proud he was of me. Wow…how could I not like him? When I was sixteen years old, he drove me to Hartselle and waited for me to take my driver's license exam. I used his 1947 Chevrolet coupe to take the driving test. After I had passed both exams, he told me to get in and drive. We drove to a local café; he bought me a hamburger and a cold drink. I was on cloud nine.

Mrs. Louie was the best cook. So many times I showed up at their table uninvited and she always made room for me. They had one of the first televisions and every one of the neighbors was welcome to come on a Saturday night to watch shows like "The Honeymooners," "Gun Smoke," and wrestling. On a number of occasions, they would all go to bed before wrestling came on. She would say to me, "When this is over, turn it off and make sure the door is locked when you leave."

John Jr. taught me how to drive their model 40 John Deere tractor. Martha Gale taught me how to drive their pick-up truck, and when I did not do something just right, she would make me stop and get in the back. I would have to eat dust until we got back to their house.

Billy Wayne, Pete, Cicero, and I played basketball together. A homemade back board, the hoop was crude, there was no net, and we played for hours. We all went swimming in the Price Hole and had the best time. I will never forget how much fun we had and how good the Ellenburg family was to all of us kids.

Mr. and Mrs. Earwood lived just a mile farther up the road. We walked by their house a lot on the way to Hulaco. Mrs. Earwood would always have something nice to say to me as I walked by, and she always waved. What I remember most about them was that they all loved music and were very good musicians. They were a proud family, good people, and great neighbors.

General and Mrs. Belle Bolding owned the next house south. See his story in Chapter 10.

Mrs. Essie Densmore lived north and east across the creek and up the road with her husband and family. Mrs. Essie rode the school bus to school and then back home. She was in charge of our lunch room at school. No matter where you saw her or what she was doing, she always, always had a wonderful smile and a kind word. I think everyone who knew her loved her. My sister Fran still talks about how much she enjoyed seeing her every day at school. Fran said it was like a breath of fresh air each time they talked; she was always smiling and so easy to talk to. All the Densmores were the best of people, hard workers, fun to talk to, and great neighbors.

Mr. Ed Jarrett and his wife, Mrs. Sue, were our neighbors to the south. Mr. Ed. was a fox hunter. I believed he knew just everything you needed to know about hunting dogs. He knew how to train them, how to take care of them, and how much each dog was worth. He was so easy to talk to; I always had the best time when I was at their house. Mrs. Sue was tall and slim; she was a great country cook and made the best cornbread ever.

Mr. Boyd Alvin and Mrs. Pauline Flack and their family were great neighbors. They lived just up the road from the Jarretts. Mrs. Pauline was one of my mom's best friends. They were a large family and such good neighbors. She was the only neighbor who gave me a whooping and boy did she give me a good one….She had no mercy on me. One time, two of her boys were in a pretty good fight. I stepped in and tried to break it up. Well, that didn't work as pretty soon all three of us were fighting. She came out and separated us then got a belt and gave her two boys a good whooping, and then she said, "You're next." I learned a good lesson then; never get involved in a family feud. Mrs. Pauline wrote to me often when I first went into the army and was always encouraging me, in her words, to "make something out of myself." She was a hardworking, no-nonsense type of lady.

Not too far up the road, Mr. and Mrs. Oval Light lived. Their daughter Helen was in my class and was one of the most intelligent students in our school. We still talk from time to time. I also played basketball with their son Max. Mr. Oval was one of our insurance men and was so easy to get along with.

I do not know anyone who ever had a bad word to say about Mr. Jimmy and Mrs. Mae Moon. When you met Mr. Jimmy and Mrs. Mae, you would know automatically that they were a Christian couple. You could just tell. They loved people, they loved each other, and they loved their church. Both were quiet, soft-spoken, easy to talk to, and always—I mean always—had a smile for you. They practiced what they preached. Mrs. Mae took a liking to us kids. She was always telling us how important it was for us to always do the right thing. There were times in my life that I didn't do the right thing; I was hoping that she would never find out.

Mr. Hubert Moore had one of the first hay balers in our community. He went all over baling hay for the local farmers. I remember someone saying that, no matter what, Mr. Hubert always showed up on time. If he said he would be there by nine in the morning, you could look down the road at quarter to nine and see him driving his tractor with the baler behind. I liked that. One time he showed me how to stack hay on the hay rack so that it would stay put. I was fifteen years old and really wanted to do a good job. He said, "I will show you one time," as if to say, "Get it right the first time." The bales weighed around eighty pounds; I didn't weigh a whole lot more. After a day working with him, you had no trouble sleeping at night. He was a good farmer with a good head on his shoulders.

One time Mr. Hubert was baling hay for one of our neighbors and he needed some extra help; my parents said okay. I was on the hay rack stacking hay with a guy by the name of Tommy. The bales were heavy and it was hot. Tommy could not talk plain and, to make it worse, he stuttered. I could never understand what he was talking about. Tommy was a really hard worker and if you bragged on him, he would really go at it. I liked him. He was funny—that is, if I could figure out what he was saying. Mr. Hubert told me to keep up with Tommy and watch how he stacked the bales. Tommy now got into high gear; he would carry two bales at a time and, with one arm, throw them all the way to the top. He made me look like a weakling. But the worst thing was Tommy chewed tobacco and, at times, when he spit, his aim was off. Some of that stuff was hitting me in the face. I said, "Tommy, you are spitting on me." Without hesitating, and very plainly, he said, "Duck." I was thinking about finding something and jabbing him in the rear end.

Mr. Hershel Latham and Mr. Jake Walker were the owners of the Hulaco General Store. In a lot of ways they were the lifeline of the community. They had just about everything you would ever need for farming, food, clothing, feed, and a hundred other things that we used in the household and farm. These two guys would bend over backwards to help others. This was the place to be on a Saturday afternoon. They made things easier for us, and no matter what we needed for the farm, they had it. This is where most of the neighbors gathered. We could always count on these two great guys. They ran the best general store ever. The Hulaco store is still open today but now as an antique store. No matter where you live, it is worth the drive just to see all the items that are for sale in this grand old general store. Mr. Dennis Buckelew is now the owner. You will still get the best service with a great smile.

I grew up in the very best of times with some of the most wonderful people who lived in our neighborhood.

The Thompsons, Armstrongs, Carters, Briscoes, Humphries, Whisenants, Ryans, Browns, Crawford's, Nunnelleys all lived within a couple of miles. Their kids went to the same small country school at Ryan and they traded at the general store at Hulaco. All were just plain good folks trying to make a living there on those dusty country roads in Morgan County, Alabama. They were the best people ever.

All of these people helped form the very foundation of my life. I learned something good and useful from each family and person. Living in the hollow.......So many great memories of Rural Route One.

I am among all men most richly blessed.

William McDaniel McCollum

Made in the USA
Charleston, SC
10 March 2014